THE JOHN DANZ LECTURES

The John Danz Lectures
Also available in this series

The Human Crisis by Julian Huxley
Of Men and Galaxies by Fred Hoyle
The Challenge of Science by George Boas
Of Molecules and Men by Francis Crick
Nothing But or Something More by Jacquetta Hawkes

HOW MUSICAL IS MAN?

JOHN BLACKING

UNIVERSITY OF WASHINGTON PRESS

SEATTLE AND LONDON

A tape recording of Venda music, prepared by the author, is available from the publisher. Included are performances of some of the musical examples in the book, as well as additional, complementary material. A descriptive listing of the items recorded accompanies the tape. 1 7-inch reel, 2-track monaural, 61 minutes, 7½ ips. $12.50

Copyright © 1973 by the University of Washington Press
Second printing, 1974
Washington Paperback edition, 1974

Printed in the United States of America

Library of Congress Cataloging in Publication Data

Blacking, John.
   How musical is man?
   (The John Danz lectures)
   1. Musical ability.   2. Ethnomusicology.
I. Title.   II. Series
ML3838.B6   780'.1   72-6710
ISBN 0-295-95218-0
ISBN 0-295-95338-1 (pbk.)

Excerpts from Benjamin Britten's *War Requiem* are reproduced by permission of Boosey & Hawkes Music Publishers Ltd.; from Gustav Mahler's Ninth Symphony and the "Abschied" from *Song of the Earth* by permission of Universal Edition (London) Ltd.; from Mahler's Tenth Symphony by permission of G. Schirmer, 140 Strand, London, WC2R 1HH, and © copyright 1966 by Associated Music Publishers, Inc., New York, used by permission. Examples from Deryck Cooke's *The Language of Music* are reproduced by permission of Oxford University Press.

All photographs are by the author.

To Meyer Fortes

THE JOHN DANZ LECTURES

IN OCTOBER, 1961, Mr. John Danz, a Seattle pioneer, and his wife, Jessie Danz, made a substantial gift to the University of Washington to establish a perpetual fund to provide income to be used to bring to the University of Washington each year "... distinguished scholars of national and international reputation who have concerned themselves with the impact of science and philosophy on man's perception of a rational universe." The fund established by Mr. and Mrs. Danz is now known as the John Danz Fund, and the scholars brought to the University under its provisions are known as John Danz Lecturers or Professors.

Mr. Danz wisely left to the Board of Regents of the University of Washington the identification of the special fields in science, philosophy, and other disciplines in which lectureships may be established. His major concern and interest were that the fund would enable the University of Washington to bring to the campus some of the truly great scholars and thinkers of the world.

Mr. Danz authorized the Regents to expend a portion of the income from the fund to purchase special collections of books, documents, and other scholarly materials needed to reinforce the effectiveness of the extraordinary lectureships and professorships. The terms of the gift also provided for the publication and dissemination, when this seems appropriate, of the lectures given by the John Danz Lecturers.

Through this book, therefore, another John Danz Lecturer speaks to the people and scholars of the world, as he has spoken to his audiences at the University of Washington and in the Pacific Northwest community.

PREFACE

This is not a scholarly study of human musicality, so much as an attempt to reconcile my experiences of music making in different cultures. I present new information that is a result of my research in African music, as well as some facts that are familiar to anyone brought up in the tradition of European "art" music; but my conclusions and suggestions are exploratory. They express the dilemma of a musician who has become a professional anthropologist, and it is for this reason that I dedicate the book to Meyer Fortes. In 1952, when I was devoting far more time to music than to my courses in anthropology, he sent me to Paris to study ethnomusicology under André Schaeffner during a summer vacation. But another five years passed before I began to glimpse the possibilities of an anthropology of music. Even after a year's intensive fieldwork, I tended to regard African music as something "other"; and this attitude would be reinforced when I listened to a tape of *Wozzeck* or some of Webern's music in my tent, or whenever there was a piano available and I could immerse myself in Bach, or Chopin, or Mozart.

It was the Venda of South Africa who first broke down some of my prejudices. They introduced me to a new world of musical experience and to a deeper understanding of "my own" music. I had been brought up to understand music as a system of ordering sound, in which a cumulative set of rules and an increasing range of permissible sound patterns had been invented and developed by Europeans who were considered to have had exceptional musical ability. By associating different "sonic objects" with various personal experiences, by hearing and playing repeatedly the music of certain approved composers, and by selective reinforcement that was supposed to be objectively aesthetic but was not unrelated to class interests, I acquired a repertoire of performing and composing techniques and musical values that were as predictably a consequence of my social and cultural environment as are the musical abilities and taste of a Venda man a convention of his society. The chief results of nearly two years' fieldwork among the Venda and of attempts to analyze my data over a period of twelve years are that I think I am beginning to understand the Venda system; I no longer understand the history and structures of European "art" music as clearly as I did; and I can see no useful distinction between the terms "folk" and "art" music, except as commercial labels.

The Venda taught me that music can never be a thing in itself, and that *all* music is folk music, in the sense that music cannot be transmitted or have meaning without associations between people. Distinctions between the surface complexity of different musical styles and techniques do not tell us anything useful about the expressive purposes and power of music, or about the intellectual organization involved in its creation. Music is too deeply concerned with human feelings and experiences in society, and its patterns are too often generated by surprising outbursts of unconscious cerebration, for it to be subject to arbitrary rules, like the rules of games. Many, if not all, of music's essential processes may be found in the constitution of the human body and in pat-

terns of interaction of human bodies in society. Thus all
music is structurally, as well as functionally, folk music. The
makers of "art" music are not innately more sensitive or
cleverer than "folk" musicians: the structures of their music
simply express, by processes similar to those in Venda music,
the numerically larger systems of interaction of folk in their
societies, the consequences of a more extensive division of
labor, and an accumulated technological tradition.

Literacy and the invention of notation are clearly important
factors that may generate extended musical structures, but
they express differences of degree, and not the difference in
kind that is implied by the distinction between "art" and
"folk" music. I have limited my examples to the music of the
Venda, because I have personal experience of it and empirical
data to support my statements. But my argument about music
in one culture seems to apply to other musical systems that
have been studied by ethnomusicologists, and particularly to
Arabic, Indian, Chinese, Japanese, and Indonesian "art"
music. I am convinced that an anthropological approach to
the study of all musical systems makes more sense of them
than analyses of the patterns of sound as things in themselves.

If my guess about the biological and social origins of music
is correct, or even only partly correct, it could affect assess-
ments of musicality and patterns of music education. Above
all, it might generate some new ideas about the role of music
in education, and its general role in societies which (like the
Venda in the context of their traditional economy) are going
to have more leisure time as automation increases. I often
wondered how it was that at my preparatory school most of
the scholarships were won by choristers, who represented
only a third of the school and missed more than a third of the
classes because of sung services and choir practice. When I
lived with the Venda, I began to understand how music can
become an intricate part of the development of mind, body,

and harmonious social relationships. These ideas are, of course, older than the writings of Boethius and Plato on music; but I hope that my own experiences may add a fresh perspective to a perennial problem.

I am deeply grateful to the Board of Regents of the University of Washington, whose invitation to deliver the John Danz Lectures has given me the opportunity to think aloud and summarize some of my findings on African music. I thank Robert Kauffman, who originally suggested that I might come, and William Bergsma, Robert Garfias, and many others, who helped me to spend a very happy and stimulating month in Seattle. In particular, I thank Naomi Pascal for her enthusiasm and advice in preparing the lectures for publication, and Cyril Ehrlich for reading the manuscript and making many useful comments; but I take full responsibility for any deficiencies in the final product. I am convinced that any creative effort is the synthesis of an individual's responses to all the good things that others have given him; and so these brief acknowledgments represent only a fraction of the gratitude I owe to all those who have helped me to appreciate and understand music.

CONTENTS

HOW MUSICAL IS MAN?

Humanly Organized Sound

ETHNOMUSICOLOGY is a comparatively new word which is widely used to refer to the study of the different musical systems of the world. Its seven syllables do not give it any aesthetic advantage over the pentasyllabic "musicology," but at least they may remind us that the people of many so-called "primitive" cultures used seven-tone scales and harmony long before they heard the music of Western Europe.

Perhaps we need a cumbersome word to restore the balance to a world of music that threatens to fly up into clouds of elitism. We need to remember that in most conservatoires they teach only one particular kind of ethnic music, and that musicology is really an ethnic musicology. A School of Music such as that at the University of Washington, which establishes a subdepartment of Ethnomusicology, Ethnic Music, or Black Music, has taken the first step toward recognizing its role in tomorrow's world of music. It has implicitly redefined its Music more modestly, as a system of musical theory and practice that emerged and developed during a certain period of European history.

More important than any arbitrary, ethnocentric divisions between Music and Ethnic Music, or between Art Music and

Folk Music, are the distinctions that different cultures and social groups make between music and nonmusic. In the long run, it is the activities of Man the Music Maker that are of more interest and consequence to humanity than the particular musical achievements of Western man. If, for example, all members of an African society are able to perform and listen intelligently to their own indigenous music, and if this unwritten music, when analyzed in its social and cultural context, can be shown to have a similar range of effects on people and to be based on intellectual and musical processes that are found in the so-called "art" music of Europe, we must ask why apparently general musical abilities should be restricted to a chosen few in societies supposed to be culturally more advanced. Does cultural development represent a real advance in human sensitivity and technical ability, or is it chiefly a diversion for elites and a weapon of class exploitation? Must the majority be made "unmusical" so that a few may become more "musical"?

Research in ethnomusicology has expanded our knowledge of the different musical systems of the world, but it has not yet brought about the reassessment of human musicality which this new knowledge demands. Ethnomusicology has the power to create a revolution in the world of music and music education, if it follows the implications of its discoveries and develops as a method, and not merely an area, of study. I believe that ethnomusicology should be more than a branch of orthodox musicology concerned with "exotic" or "folk" music: it could pioneer new ways of analyzing music and music history. Currently recognized divisions between Art Music and Folk Music are inadequate and misleading as conceptual tools. They are neither meaningful nor accurate as indices of musical differences; at best, they merely define the interests and activities of different social groups. They express the same outlook as the irregular verb, "I play music; you are a folk singer; he makes a horrible noise." We need to know what sounds and what kinds of behavior different societies have chosen to call "musical"; and until we know more about this we cannot begin to answer the question, "How musical is man?"

If studies in the psychology of music and tests of musicality have failed to reach agreement on the nature of musicality, it is probably because they have been almost exclusively ethnocentric. Thus, the contradictions that exist between the different schools of thought may be artifacts of their ethnocentricity. When the Gestalt school insists that musical talent is more than a set of specific attributes dependent upon sensory capacities, it is right; but only partly right, because its whole does not extend into the culture of which the music is a part. When opponents of the Gestalt school attach prime importance to sensory capacities, they are also right, because without certain specific capacities music could neither be perceived nor performed. But their tests, like the theories on which they are based, are also of limited value and are hardly more objective than those which may seem to be less scientific. Paradoxically, their laudable aim to be context-free and objective fails precisely because they minimize the importance of cultural experience in the selection and development of sensory capacities. For instance, a test of musical pitch based on the sounds of a General Radio beat-frequency oscillator may seem to be more scientific than one based on culturally familiar timbres, because the intensity and duration of the sounds can be exactly controlled. But the results of such a test could in fact represent a distortion of the truth, because the subjects' perception may be thrown off balance by the unfamiliar medium.

One example of the ethnocentricism of all the musical tests that I have so far encountered will serve as a general criticism, and also illustrate why we must broaden our field of investigation if we are to find out what capacities are involved in musicality. Carl Seashore's *Measures of Musical*

Talents were the first standardized tests of musical ability to be published, in 1919; and although they have been criticized, refined, and elaborated both by Seashore himself and by many other workers, testing procedures have not changed radically. The basis of the Seashore tests is discrimination of some kind. Now, because sensory discrimination is developed in culture, people may fail to express any distinction between musical intervals which they can hear, but which have no significance in their musical system. Similarly, people who use only four or five basic color terms may be able to distinguish between finer shades of color even though they may not know the special terms the manufacturers have invented in order to sell the new season's clothes. I lived for nearly two years in a rural African society, and I studied the development and expression of its members' musical ability in the context of their social and cultural experience. Music plays a very important part in the life of the Venda of the Northern Transvaal, and even white settlers who suffer from the demented logic of *apartheid* readily admit that the Venda are very musical people. But when confronted with the Seashore tests of musical talent, an outstanding Venda musician might well appear to be a tone-deaf musical moron. Because his perception of sound is basically harmonic, he might declare that two intervals a fourth or a fifth apart were the same, and that there was no difference between two apparently different patterns of melody (see Example 2). Tests of timbre and loudness would be irrelevant outside the social context of sound, and in any case the sound of the oscillator would probably turn him off instantly: since it is not sound made by a human being, it is not music.

Tests of musical ability are clearly relevant only to the cultures whose musical systems are similar to that of the tester. But I would ask further questions: How useful are musical tests even within the cultural tradition in which they are set? What do the tests test, and how far is it related to *musical* ability? How musical is the ability that finds its expression in musical composition or performance, and under what conditions can it emerge? We cannot answer the question, "How musical is man?" until we know what features of human behavior, if any, are peculiar to music. We talk freely of musical genius, but we do not know what qualities of genius are restricted to music and whether or not they might find expression in another medium. Nor do we know to what extent these qualities may be latent in all men. It may well be that the social and cultural inhibitions that prevent the flowering of musical genius are more significant than any individual ability that may seem to promote it.

The question, "How musical is man?" is related to the more general questions, "What is the nature of man?" and, "What limits are there to his cultural development?" It is part of a series of questions that we must ask about man's past and present if we are to do anything more than stumble blindly forward into the future. Although I have no final answer to the question posed by the title of the book, I hope to show in the first three chapters how research in ethnomusicology may resolve most of the problems, and, in the fourth, why the issue may be important for the future of humanity. There is so much music in the world that it is reasonable to suppose that music, like language and possibly religion, is a species-specific trait of man. Essential physiological and cognitive processes that generate musical composition and performance may even be genetically inherited, and therefore present in almost every human being. An understanding of these and other processes involved in the production of music may provide us with evidence that men are more remarkable and capable creatures than most societies ever allow them to be. This is not the fault of culture itself, but the fault of man, who mistakes the means of culture for the end, and so lives *for* culture and not *beyond* culture.

Consider the contradictions between theory and practice in

the matter of musicality in the kind of bourgeois environment in which I was raised and seemed to acquire a degree of musical competence. (I say "seemed," because an essential point of my argument is that we do not know exactly what musical competence is or how it is acquired.) Music is played while we eat and try to talk; it is played between films and at the theater; it is played as we sit in crowded airport lounges, and ominously as we wait in the plane to take off; it is played all day long on the radio; and even in church few organists allow moments of silence to intervene between different stages of the ritual. "My" society claims that only a limited number of people are musical, and yet it behaves as if all people possessed the basic capacity without which no musical tradition can exist—the capacity to listen to and distinguish patterns of sound. The makers of most films and television serials hope to appeal to large and varied audiences; and so, when they add incidental music to the dialogue and action, they implicitly assume that audiences can discern its patterns and respond to its emotional appeal, and that they will hear and understand it in the ways that its composer intended. They assume that music is a form of communication, and that in a common cultural context specific musical sequences can evoke feelings that are fearful, apprehensive, passionate, patriotic, religious, spooky, and so on.

The film makers may not be aware of the grounds for their assumptions; but we can be sure that, if experience had proved them wrong, they would have rejected all incidental and mood music as unnecessary. Instead, they seem to have shown increasing confidence in their audiences' musicality by abandoning continual background music in favor of more selective heightening of the drama. This may be only a response to the pressures of musicians' unions; but, even if this were so, film makers continue to commission composers of music, at considerable extra expense. It is interesting that these assumptions should be made by men and women whose attitudes to art and financial profit often contradict them. A producer's training in Western European culture must have taught him that not all people are musical, and that some are more musical than others. But his knowledge and experience of life lead him unconsciously to reject this theory. Capitalist dogma tells him that only a chosen few are musical, but capitalist experience reminds him that *The Sound of Music* was one of the biggest box-office draws of all time.

One explanation of this paradox comes immediately to mind. In many industrial societies, merit is generally judged according to signs of immediate productivity and profits, and postulated usefulness, within the boundaries of a given system. Latent ability is rarely recognized or nurtured, unless its bearer belongs to the right social class or happens to show evidence of what people have learned to regard as talent. Thus, children are judged to be musical or unmusical on the basis of their ability to perform music. And yet the very existence of a professional performer, as well as his necessary financial support, depends on listeners who in one important respect must be no less musically proficient than he is. They must be able to distinguish and interrelate different patterns of sound.

I am aware that many audiences before and since the composition of Haydn's *Surprise Symphony* have not listened attentively to music, and that, in a society which has invented notation, music could be handed down by a hereditary elite without any need for listeners. But if we take a world view of music, and if we consider social situations in musical traditions that have no notation, it is clear that the creation and performance of most music is generated first and foremost by the human capacity to discover patterns of sound and to identify them on subsequent occasions. Without biological processes of aural perception, and without cultural agreement among at least some human beings on what is perceived, there can be neither music nor musical communication.

The importance of creative listening is too often ignored in discussions of musical ability, and yet it is as fundamental to music as it is to language. The interesting thing about child prodigies is not so much that some children are born with apparently exceptional gifts, but that a child can respond to the organized sounds of music before he has been taught to recognize them. We know, too, that children who are not prodigies may be equally responsive, though they may not relate to music in a positive way and seek to reproduce their experience.

In societies where music is not written down, informed and accurate listening is as important and as much a measure of musical ability as is performance, because it is the only means of ensuring continuity of the musical tradition. Music is a product of the behavior of human groups, whether formal or informal: it is humanly organized sound. And, although different societies tend to have different ideas about what they regard as music, all definitions are based on some consensus of opinion about the principles on which the sounds of music should be organized. No such consensus can exist until there is some common ground of experience, and unless different people are able to hear and recognize patterns in the sounds that reach their ears.

Insofar as music is a cultural tradition that can be shared and transmitted, it cannot exist unless at least some human beings possess, or have developed, a capacity for structured listening. Musical performance, as distinct from the production of noise, is inconceivable without the perception of order in sound.

If my emphasis on the primacy of listening may seem too farfetched, consider what would happen even to a tradition of written music if mere performance were regarded as the criterion of musical ability. Musicians know that it is possible to get away with a bad or inaccurate performance with an audience that looks but does not listen; and even listening audiences can be trained to accept gross deviations from familiar scores of Chopin or Beethoven, which were at first currently fashionable but later became part of a pianistic tradition. The continuity of music depends as much on the demands of critical listeners as on a supply of performers.

When I say that music cannot exist without the perception of order in the realm of sound, I am not arguing that some kind of theory of music must precede musical composition and performance: this would obviously be untrue of most great classical compositions and of the work of so-called "folk" musicians. I am suggesting that a perception of sonic order, whether it be innate or learned, or both, must be in the mind before it emerges as music.

I deliberately use the term "sonic order" and stress experiences of external listening because I want to emphasize that any assessment of man's musicality must be based on descriptions of a distinctive and limited field of human behavior which we will provisionally call "musical." Sonic order may be created incidentally as a result of principles of organization that are nonmusical or extramusical, such as the selection of equidistantly spaced holes on a flute or frets on a stringed instrument. Similarly, an apparent lack of sonic order may express ordered arrangements of numbers, people, mathematical formulae, or any elements that can be transformed into sound, such as the application of a sine curve to an electronic machine.

If a composer tells me that I must not expect to hear any order "in the notes," but that I may observe it in patterns of circles and cones that are given to performers, or in numbers that are fed into a machine, I may prefer to call the noise reactionary magic rather than avant-garde music; but I cannot exclude it from any estimation of human musicality, even though it probably does not belong to the area of behavior that includes the music of the Bushmen, the Bemba, the Balinese, Bach, Beethoven, and Bartók. It is humanly organized sound, intended for other human ears and possibly enjoyed by the composers' friends, and thus concerned with communication and relationships between people.

This process of producing musical sound is not as modern or sophisticated as its creators might claim: it is simply an extension of the general principle that music should express aspects of human organization or humanly conditioned perceptions of "natural" organization. I observed a similar process in Zambia in 1961. Among the Nsenga of the Petauke district, boys play small *kalimba mbiras* as a diversion when they are walking or sitting alone. Analysis of the tunes they play reveals relationships between the patterns of movement of the left and right thumbs, the patterns of rhythm with which they pluck the "keys," and the patterned arrangement of the "keyboard" itself (see Figure 1). The tunes do not sound like other Nsenga music, but the two thumbs perform typically Nsenga polyrhythms, which in other contexts would be performed by more than one player. A similar instrument called the *ndimba* has a different "keyboard" more suited to melodic accompaniment than to patterned doodling. The men who play this instrument are usually public entertainers, who sing with or to large audiences. Though their music often sounds simpler than that which the boys play, it is in fact more musical in construction, since the patterned relationship between thumb movement and "keyboard" is subordinate to the requirements of a song, with words and a form that allow others to sing with the instrument. Some of the boys' tunes may be more experimental and avant-garde, but they do not concern many people, since they lack a quality the Nsenga seem to desire of their music, namely, the power to bring people together in brotherhood.

It is possible to give more than one analysis of any piece of music, and an enormous amount of print is devoted to doing just this. But it ought to be possible to produce exact analyses that indicate where musical and extramusical proc-

Transcriptions of three Nsenga melodies for *kalimba*

Layout of the "keys" of a 14-note *kalimba* (A) and a 14-note *ndimba* (B).
(i): Approximate pitches of the scales most commonly used (transposed).
(ii): Numbering of "keys" from left to right of the "keyboard." (iii): "Keys"
numbered symmetrically according to their use in contrary motion by the
right and left thumbs. Shaded "keys" and underlined numbers above and below the music staff indicate pitches in the upper manual of the "keyboard."

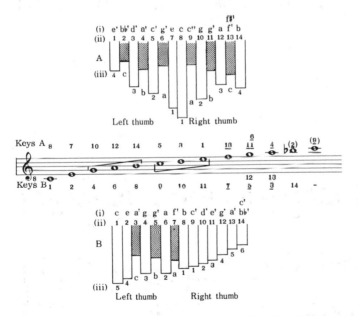

FIGURE 1. *Comparison of melodies and "keyboards"* of kalimba
and ndimba *mbiras, played by the Nsenga of Petauke, Zambia,
illustrating the cultural and physical origins of musical sound.*

Rhythmic foundations of *kalimba* melodies, as revealed by analyses of parts played by left and right thumbs

FIGURE 1 *continued*

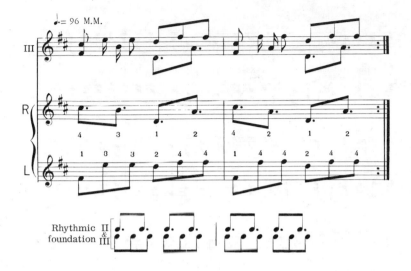

Rhythmic II
foundation III

Analysis of *ndimba* melody

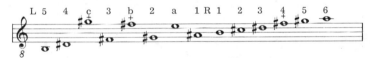

FIGURE 1 *continued*

FIGURE 1 *continued*

esses are employed, and precisely what they are and why they were used. At some level of analysis, all musical behavior is structured, whether in relation to biological, psychological, sociological, cultural, or purely musical processes; and it is the task of the ethnomusicologist to identify all processes that are relevant to an explanation of musical sound.

Figure 2 shows a musical passage that can be interpreted in at least two ways. It is one of a number of short repeated figures that occur in a series of tunes played by a Nande (or Konjo) flute player from Butembo, in Zaire, and it is clear from the musical context that it gives the player pleasure and expresses fundamental principles of musical structure. What is not clear from the music alone is the nature of these principles. A listener trained in European ethnic music may hear movement away from and back to a tone center, which he would describe as a tonic-dominant-tonic sequence. More generally, in terms Hindemith and others have used, this could be described as a musical sequence expressing relaxation-tension-relaxation. The Nande musician may also conceive the passage as movement away from and back to a tone center, since much African music is structured in this way, though he would not think specifically in terms of tonic and dominant relationships. But if we consider his performance in relation to the physical experience of stopping holes with the fingers, the tonal relationships acquire a different meaning. The physical relaxation of throwing the fingers off the flute produces a tone that is harmonically tense, while the physical tension of stopping certain holes produces a tone that is harmonically relaxed.

I do not know which of these interpretations of the music is right in the context of Nande society and the musicianship of the particular performer, Katsuba Mwongolo, or whether there is another explanation. But I am sure that there is ultimately only one explanation and that this could be discov-

Musical phrase used in flute music from Butembo

Stopping of flute from Butembo, and tones produced

● represents stopped hole.
○ represents open hole.

		1st finger ·· ·· ··	●	●	●	●	○
R.H.	{						
		3rd finger ·· ·· ··	●	●	●	○	○
L.H.	{	1st finger ·· ·· ··	●	●	○	○	○
		3rd finger ·· ·· ··	●	○	○	○	○
			d″	e″	f″	g″	a″

Transformation	"Language"	MODEL	"Language"	Transformation
	HARMONIC		PHYSICAL (stopping of flute holes: fingering)	
Tone in the musical phrase				Tone in the musical phrase
A	Dominant	TENSION	1	G
G	Tonic	RELAXATION	0	A
A	Dominant	TENSION	1	G
G	Tonic	RELAXATION	0	A

FIGURE 2. *Two possible interpretations of the same musical passage, using a tension/relaxation model and harmonic and physical "languages," respectively.*

ered by a context-sensitive analysis of the music in culture. When I analyzed the flute melodies in 1955, I was working with annotated recordings and a specimen instrument which I learned to play. I had no firsthand experience of the culture of the performer and no evidence of its musical system, since very few recordings were available.

I can be more confident about the analysis of the balance

Two Venda girls play alto drums (mirumba) *at the
domba initiation. They sway their bodies from side to
side, keeping a steady rhythm so that the drumbeat is
part of a total body movement.*

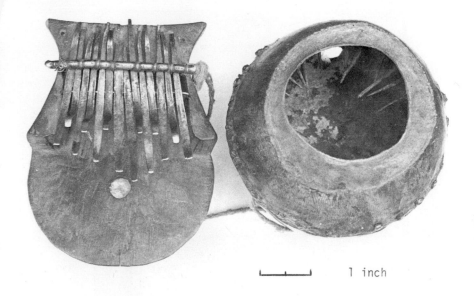

1 inch

Fourteen-note kalimba mbira *of the Nsenga of Zambia.*

A beer-drink at a headman's homestead.

The village of a Venda chief at Thengwe. The houses are occupied by his wives, relatives, and councilors. The big tree slightly to the left of center shades the khoro, meeting place of the council and scene of music and dancing.

Masked dancer (muhwira) *at the Venda girls'* sungwi *initiation.*

A Venda novice performs a special ndayo movement at her
tshikanda initiation. Note the contrast in response between her two
companions and the married women running the proceedings

Ngoma dza midzimu, Venda dance of spirit possession. The
hunchbacked girl who is dancing in the arena will not be possessed
because she does not belong to this particular cult group. Those
who have been possessed wear a special uniform and shake
hand rattles.

Venda girls practice the first part of the tshigombela *dance.*

Venda girls dancing "solo" (u gaya) during the second part of a tshigombela *dance.*

between physical and musical factors in generating the tunes played on the Nsenga *kalimba* and *ndimba mbiras,* because I worked in Zambia in 1961 with the performers and learned to play the tunes (very badly), I observed the different contexts of performance, and I heard and recorded scores of other pieces of Nsenga music. Only by assembling musical and extramusical information was it possible to discover what was "in the notes."

It is possible to improvise musical tests in the field; and these may provide the only means of discovering or confirming the principles that generate musical composition. For example, Venda youths play duets on ocarinas, called *zwipoto-liyo,* which they make from small fruits of varying diameters (ca. 4.5 to 7 cms), in which they have cut one large hole for blowing and two for stopping with the fingers. The tones that can be played on the ocarinas vary according to the size of the spheres, and their pitch can be modified by the blowing of the performer. For the duets, players select pairs that "sound good," and so their choice indicates what musical principles they hope to express in the duets. I devised a test in which two youths selected the most satisfactory of all combinations of six differently tuned ocarinas; the sound of the duets played on these instruments, therefore, revealed tonal and harmonic principles that are important in ocarina music in particular and Venda music in general. Figure 3 shows three such patterns, with their root progressions and harmonic sequence.

These three examples illustrate problems that exist in analyzing the music of any composer or culture. They also emphasize the dangers of comparing different music solely on the basis of its sound. Even though the meaning of music rests ultimately "in the notes" that human ears perceive, there can be several possible structural interpretations of any pattern of sound, and an almost infinite number of individual responses to its structure, depending on the cultural back-

Three Venda ocarina duets

FIGURE 3. *Tonal and harmonic principles in Venda ocarina music.*

Scale diagram of two Venda ocarinas, made from hollowed fruits (A: of *Strychnos spinosa Lam.*, the wild orange; B: of *Oncoba spinosa Forsk.*)

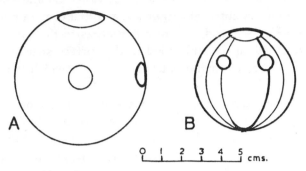

FIGURE 3 *continued*

ground and current emotional state of its listeners.

However, the number of possible structural interpretations can be greatly reduced when the musical system of a single composer or culture is considered in its total cultural context. Even when a system is clearly articulated, a structural explanation in terms of that system may be incomplete. For example, we know much about the theory and practice of harmony in the European "art" music of the nineteenth century, but when we analyze the music of Hector Berlioz it is useful to know that he often worked out harmonic procedures on a guitar, and that the structure of the instrument influenced many of his chord sequences.

Let me illustrate the analytical problem further by an analogy from structural linguistics. In doing this, I am not suggesting that ethnomusicology should use the methods of linguistics, though the aims of musical and linguistic analysis may be similar. I see no reason to assume that music is a kind of language, or that it has any special structural relationships with language, or that language processes are necessarily more fundamental than other human cultural activities. However, analyses of language behavior by Eric Lenneberg and by Noam Chomsky and his associates point to features that

have parallels in music. I do not refer so much to the obvious
fact that the sound *si* can have different structural and semantic significance in different languages, and that even in English
the words *sea, see,* and *see* are different, as to the variety of
structures that can be embedded in the surface structures of
a language, that is, in the patterns of words which we hear
and to which we respond.

English speakers generally understand strings of words
according to the context in which they are heard. Thus, as
Lenneberg points out, the string "they-are-boring-students"
has two possible syntactic interpretations which are directly
related to two possible semantic interpretations. The sentence
can be either a comment by faculty on students—$\left|\{\right|$ [(They)]
[(are) ((boring) (students))] $\}$ —in which "boring" is an ad-
jective; or it can be a comment by students on faculty—
$\{$ [(They)] [(are boring) (students)] $|\}$—in which "boring" is
an inflected verb form. In many cases, however, there is not
a one-to-one relationship between syntactic and semantic interpretations. Chomsky has shown that at the surface level
the structure of the gerundial phrase "the shooting of the
hunters" may be a transformation of either the active sentence "hunters shoot," or the passive "hunters are shot."

It is because of this kind of relationship between deep and
surface structures that we cannot regard language as a matter
of fitting words into grammatical slots according to learned
patterns, regardless of the cognitive processes that underlie
the patterns. There is a world of difference between the active
sentence "John is eager to please" and the passive "John is
easy to please," although on the surface only one word has
been changed. Similarly, we cannot substitue *any* similar verb
form for "shooting" without considering the semantic implications, which in turn bring into play different structural
principles. In some contexts I can talk of "the eating of the
hunters" in the same way as "the shooting of the hunters,"
but in all contexts known to me "the drinking of the hunters"

can have only one structural and semantic interpretation. Logical possibilities must always be considered, however, and in some cultures the ambiguity of phrases such as "the singing of the hunters" or "the dancing of the hunters," which ought to be transformations only of active sentences, may be resolved by the concept that a man can "be sung" or "be danced."

Musical structures, like strings of words, can be interpreted as the results of fitting tones into slots according to the rules of a musical grammar. But if the deep structures are ignored, confusion may arise. A humorous consequence of such an approach to musical analysis is quoted by Deryck Cooke in his book *The Language of Music* ([London: Oxford University Press, 1959], Ex. 73, p. 186). A friend of his "confidently assumed" that "the once-popular comic song 'Yes, we have no bananas (we have no bananas today)'" was generated in the following way:

Example 1

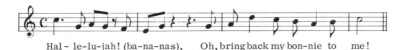

Hal - le-lu-jah! (ba-na-nas),   Oh, bring back my bon-nie to   me!

A more serious illustration of the importance of deep structures in the analysis of music is provided by two different versions of a Venda children's song, *Funguvhu tanzwa mulomo!* (see Example 2). The two melodies are described as "the same" because they are melodic transformations of the same deep structure, which is an essentially "harmonic" sequence, given rhythmic impetus and contour by a string of words. The tones of one melody are the harmonic equivalents of the other.

The first problem in assessing human musicality is also the central issue in musicology and ethnomusicology. It is the

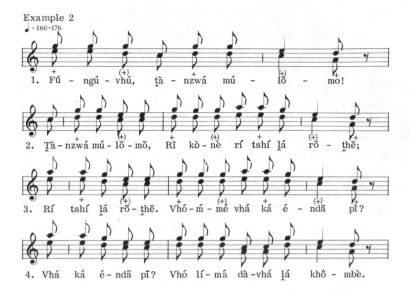

Example 2

1. Fú - ngú - vhú, t̯à - nzwá mú - lō - mo!
2. T̯à - nzwá mú - lō - mō, Rì kò - nè rí tshí ḻá rō - t̯hē;
3. Rí tshí ḻá rō - t̯hē. Vhó - m̄ - mé vhá ká é - ndā pī?
4. Vhá ká é - ndā pī? Vhó lí - má dà -vhá ḻá khô - mbè.

problem of describing what happens in a piece of music. We cannot yet explain what we already know intuitively as a result of experience in culture, namely, the essential differences between the music of Haydn and Mozart, or of the Flathead and the Sioux Indians. It is not enough to know the distinctive features of Mozart's piano concertos or of Beethoven's orchestration: we want to know exactly how and why Beethoven is Beethoven, Mozart is Mozart, and Haydn is Haydn. Every composer has a basic cognitive system that sets its stamp on his major works, regardless of the ensembles for which they were written. This cognitive system includes all cerebral activity involved in his motor coordination, feelings, and cultural experiences, as well as his social, intellectual, and musical activities. An accurate and comprehensive description of a composer's cognitive system will, therefore, provide the most fundamental and powerful explanation of the patterns that his music takes. Similarly, the musical styles current in a society will be best understood as expressions of cognitive processes that may be observed to operate in the formation of other structures. When we know how these cognitive processes work in producing the patterns of sound different societies call "music," we shall be in a better position to find out how musical man is.

The study of music in culture is what Alan Merriam advocated in his important book, *The Anthropology of Music* (Evanston, Ill.: Northwestern University Press, 1964), but ethnomusicologists have yet to produce systematic cultural analyses of music that explain how a musical system is part of other systems of relationships within a culture. It is not enough to identify a characteristic musical style in its own terms and view it in relation to its society (to paraphrase a definition of one of the aims of ethnomusicology by Mantle Hood, who has done more for the subject than almost any other living ethnomusicologist). We must recognize that no musical style has "its own terms": its terms are the terms of its society and culture, and of the bodies of the human beings who listen to it, and create and perform it.

We can no longer study music as a thing in itself when research in ethnomusicology makes it clear that musical things are not always strictly musical, and that the expression of tonal relationships in patterns of sound may be secondary to extramusical relationships which the tones represent. We may agree that music is sound that is organized into socially accepted patterns, that music making may be regarded as a form of learned behavior, and that musical styles are based on what man has chosen to select from nature as a part of his cultural expression rather than on what nature has imposed on him. But the nature from which man has selected his musical styles is not only external to him; it includes his own nature—his psychophysical capacities and the ways in which these have been structured by his experiences of interaction with people and things, which are part of the adaptive process of maturation in culture. We do not know which of these psychophysical capacities, apart from hearing, are essential for music making, or whether any of them are specific to music. It seems that musical activities are associated with specific parts of the brain, and that these are not the same as the language centers. But we shall never know what to look for until we study the creative processes that are present even in a learned performance of music, much as they are present in the sentences of a learned language.

Ethnomusicology's claim to be a new method of analyzing music and music history must rest on an assumption not yet generally accepted, namely, that because music is humanly organized sound, there ought to be a relationship between patterns of human organization and the patterns of sound produced as a result of human interaction. I am chiefly interested in the analysis of musical structures because this is the first step toward understanding musical processes and hence assessing musicality. We may never be able to understand exactly how another person feels about a piece of music, but we can perhaps understand the structural factors that generate the feelings. Attention to music's function in society is necessary only in so far as it may help us to explain the structures. Although I shall discuss the uses and effects of music, I am concerned primarily with what music is, and not what is is used for. If we know what it is, we might be able to use and develop it in all kinds of ways that have not yet been imagined, but which may be inherent in it.

The sound may be the object, but man is the subject; and the key to understanding music is in the relationships existing between subject and object, the activating principle of organization. Stravinsky expressed this with characteristic insight when he said of his own ethnic music: "Music is given to us with the sole purpose of establishing an order in things, including, and particularly, the coordination between *man* and *time*" (*Chronicle of My Life* [London: Gollancz, 1936], p. 83). Every culture has its own rhythm, in the sense that conscious experience is ordered into cycles of seasonal change, physical growth, economic enterprise, genealogical depth or width, life and afterlife, political succession, or any other recurring features that are given significance. We may say that ordinary daily experience takes place in a world of actual time. The essential quality of music is its power to create another world of virtual time.

In the musical system of the Venda, it is rhythm that distinguishes song *(u imba)* from speech *(u amba)*, so that patterns of words that are recited to a regular meter are called "songs." Both Stravinsky and the Venda insist that music involves man. The regular beats of an engine or a pump may sound like the beats of a drum, but no Venda would regard them as music or expect to be moved by them, because their order is not directly produced by human beings. The sound of electronic instruments or of a Moog synthesizer would not be excluded from their realm of musical experience as long as it was only the timbre and not the method of ordering that was outside human control. Venda music is founded not on melody, but on a rhythmical stirring of the whole body of which singing is but one extension. Therefore, when we seem to hear a rest between two drumbeats, we must realize that for the player it is not a rest: each drumbeat is the part of a total body movement in which the hand or a stick strikes the drum skin.

These principles apply in the children's song *Tshidula tsha Musingadi* (Example 3), which for the Venda is music, and not speech or poetry.

One might expect the beat to fall on the syllables -*du, tsha,* and -*nga-,* which are stressed in performance. But if people clap to the song, they clap on the syllables *Tshi-, -la, -si-,* and -*di,* so that there is not a rest on the fourth beat, but a total pattern of four beats that can be repeated any number of times, but never less than once if it is to qualify as "song" and not "speech."

Example 3

♩=108-112 *Parlando*

1. Tshi - du - la   tsha Mu - si - nga - di!
2. Vha - ko - ma   vha   tshi ya   Dza - ta,

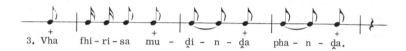

3. Vha   fhi - ri - sa   mu - di - n - da   pha - n - da.

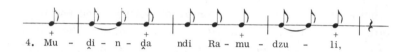

4. Mu - di - n - da   ndi   Ra - mu - dzu - li,

Venda music is overtly political in that it is performed in a variety of political contexts and often for specific political purposes. It is also political in the sense that it may involve people in a powerful shared experience within the framework of their cultural experience and thereby make them more aware of themselves and of their responsibilities toward each other. "*Muthu ndi muthu nga vhaṅwe,*" the Venda say: "Man is man because of his associations with other men." Venda music is not an escape from reality; it is an adventure into reality, the reality of the world of the spirit. It is an experience of becoming, in which individual consciousness is nurtured within the collective consciousness of the community and hence becomes the source of richer cultural forms. For example, if two drummers play exactly the same surface rhythm, but maintain an individual, inner difference of tempo or beat, they produce something more than their individual efforts. Thus, the combination of a straightforward beat played by two people at different tempi produces:

Example 4

A combination of iambic rhythms with different main beat can produce:

Example 5

Other combinations are illustrated in Figure 4, which shows how the same surface structure may be produced by different processes, involving one, two, or three players.

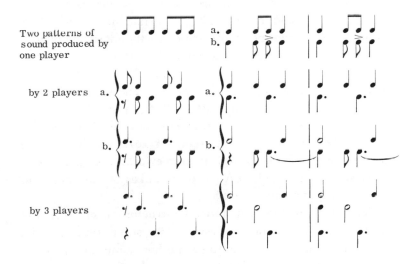

FIGURE 4. *Different ways in which one, two, or three players may produce the same surface structures of music.*

To describe these differently organized patterns of sound as the same "sonic objects" simply because they *sound* the same would be grossly misleading. Even to recognize the way in which the sounds are produced and to describe some of them as examples of polyrhythm would be inadequate in the context of Venda music. They must be described first in terms of cognitive and behavioral processes that belong to the pattern of Venda culture.

A cultural analysis of some of the rhythms in Figure 4 would not be one which simply points out that they are used in such-and-such a way on a stated variety of occasions. It would not be a program note outlining the context of the music, but an analytical device describing its structure as an expression of cultural patterns. Thus, performances by combinations of two or three players of rhythms that can in fact be played by one are not musical gimmicks: they express concepts of individuality in community, and of social, temporal, and spatial balance, which are found in other features of Venda culture and other types of Venda music. Rhythms such as these cannot be performed correctly unless the players are their own conductors and yet at the same time submit to the rhythm of an invisible conductor. This is the kind of shared experience which the Venda seek and express in their music making, and an analysis of their music that ignored these facts would be as incomplete as an analysis of Monteverdi's *Vespro della Beata Vergine* of 1610 which failed to take account of the liturgical framework, the composer's early sacred works, his service to the dukes of Gonzaga, and his early experiments in opera.

Functional analyses of musical structure cannot be detached from structural analyses of its social function: the function of tones in relation to each other cannot be explained adequately as part of a closed system without reference to the structures of the sociocultural system of which the musical system is a part, and to the biological system to which all music makers belong. Ethnomusicology is not only an area study concerned with exotic music, nor a musicology of the ethnic—it is a discipline that holds out hope for a deeper understanding of all music. If some music can be analyzed and understood as tonal expressions of human experience in the context of different kinds of social and cultural organization, I see no reason why all music should not be analyzed in the same way.

Music in Society and Culture

I HAVE DESCRIBED music as humanly organized sound. I have argued that we ought to look for relationships between patterns of human organization and the patterns of sound produced as a result of organized interaction. I reinforced this general statement by referring to the concepts of music shared by the Venda of the Northern Transvaal. The Venda also share the experience of music *making,* and without this experience there would be very little music. The production of the patterns of sound which the Venda call music depends, first, on the continuity of the social groups who perform it and, second, on the way the members of those groups relate to each other.

In order to find out what music is and how musical man is, we need to ask who listens and who plays and sings in any given society, and why. This is a sociological question, and situations in different societies can be compared without any reference to the surface forms of music because we are concerned only with its function in social life. In this respect, there may be no significant differences between Black Music, Country and Western Music, Rock and Pop Music, Operas, Symphonic Music, or Plainchant. What turns one man off

may turn another man on, not because of any absolute quality in the music itself but because of what the music has come
to mean to him as a member of a particular culture or social
group. We must also remember that, while we may have our
own personal preferences, we cannot judge the effectiveness
of music or the feelings of musicians by what seems to happen to people. If an old, blind master of Venda initiation
listens in silence to a recording of the *domba* initiation song,
we cannot rate the music more or less effective than a recording of Spokes Mashiyane's penny whistle band from Johannesburg, which bores him but excites his grandson. We
cannot say that the Kwakiutl are more emotional than the
Hopi because their style of dancing looks more ecstatic to
our eyes. In some cultures, or in certain types of music and
dancing within a culture, emotions may be deliberately inter-
nalized, but they are not necessarily less intense. A man's
mystical or psychedelic experiences may not be seen or felt
by his neighbors, but they cannot be dismissed as irrelevant
to his life in society.

The same criteria of judgment should be applied to apparent differences in the surface complexity of music, which we
tend to see in the same terms as that of other cultural products. Because the growing complexity of cars, airplanes, and
many other machines can be related to their efficiency as
means of communication, it is often assumed that technical
development in music and the arts must likewise be a sign
of deeper or better expression. I suggest that the popularity
of some Indian music in Europe and America is not unrelated
to the fact that it seems to be technically brilliant as well as
pleasing to the ear, and that it is accompanied by profound
philosophizing. When I try to interest my students in the
sounds of African music, I know that I too tend to draw their
attention to technical feats in performance, because these are
more immediately appreciated. And yet the simplicity or
complexity of the music is ultimately irrelevant: the equation

should not be LESS = BETTER or MORE = BETTER, but MORE or
LESS = DIFFERENT. It is the *human* content of the humanly organized sound that "sends" people. Even if this emerges as
an exquisite turn of melody or harmony, as a "sonic object"
if you like, it still began as the thought of a sensitive human
being, and it is this sensitivity that may arouse (or not) the
feelings of another human being, in much the same way that
magnetic impulses convey a telephone conversation from one
speaker to another.

The issue of musical complexity becomes important only
when we try to assess human musicality. Suppose I argue
that, because there are some societies whose members are as
competent in music as all people are in language, music may
be a species-specific trait of man. Someone will almost certainly retort that evidence of a widespread distribution of
listening and performing ability among the Venda and other
apparently musical societies should not be compared with the
limited distribution of musical ability in, say, England because
the complexity of English music is such that only a few could
master it. In other words, if English music were as elementary
as Venda music, then of course the English would seem to
be as universally musical as the Venda! The broader implica-
tion of this argument is that technological development
brings about a degree of social exclusion: being a passive audience is the price that some must pay for membership in a
superior society whose superiority is sustained by the exceptional ability of a chosen few. The technical level of what is
defined as musicality is therefore raised, and some people
must be branded as unmusical. It is on such assumptions that
musical ability is fostered or anesthetized in many modern
industrial societies. These assumptions are diametrically op-
posed to the Venda idea that all normal human beings are
capable of musical performance.

The issue of musical complexity is irrelevant in any con-
sideration of universal musical competence. First, within a

single musical system greater surface complexity may be like an extension of vocabulary, which does not alter the basic priniciples of a grammar and is meaningless apart from them. Second, in comparing different systems we cannot assume that *surface* complexity is either musically or cognitively more complex. In any case, the mind of man is infinitely more complex than anything produced by particular men or cultures. Above all, the functional effectiveness of music seems to be more important to listeners than its surface complexity or simplicity. What is the use of being the greatest pianist in the world, or of writing the cleverest music, if nobody wants to listen to it? What is the human use of inventing or using new sounds just for their own sake? Do new sounds mean anything in Venda culture, for instance, in terms of new groups and social change? Why sing or dance or play at all? Why bother to improve *musical* technique if the aim of performance is to share a *social* experience?

The functions of music in society may be the decisive factors promoting or inhibiting latent musical ability, as well as affecting the choice of cultural concepts and materials with which to compose music. We shall not be able to explain the principles of composition and the effects of music until we understand better the relationship between musical and human experience. If I describe some of the functions of music in Venda society, perhaps the new knowledge may stimulate a better understanding of similar processes in other societies. This has certainly been my own experience. Since my initial stay of two years in the Sibasa district between 1956 and 1958, and as a result of subsequent fieldwork in other parts of Africa, I have come to understand my own society more clearly and I have learned to appreciate my own music better. I do not know whether or not my analyses of Venda music are correct: I have benefited greatly by the criticisms of Venda who have been good enough to discuss my evidence and conclusions, but there may be other interpretations that have so far escaped us. Whatever the ultimate judgment on my analyses of Venda music, I hope that my discoveries may play a small part in restoring the conditions of dignity and freedom in which their musical tradition originally developed.

There are about three hundred thousand Venda, and most of them live in the undeveloped rural area that was left to them when white colonists took the rest of their land for farming and mining. Compared with over twelve million black South Africans, divided almost equally among the Zulu, Xhosa, and Sotho-Tswana language groups, the Venda may seem insignificant. And yet the white South African government has shown great interest in them and has held an important military exercise in their so-called homeland. For the Venda live in and around the Zoutpansberg Mountains, just south of the Limpopo River, the northern boundary of the white Republic of South Africa. Since I was there in 1958, more and more whites have been settling on land that was once reserved for blacks.

In 1899 the Venda became the last of the South Africans to submit to Boer rule. They are well placed to become the first to achieve their full freedom. The ancestors of some Venda clans lived in Venda long before whites landed in the Cape, and they managed to retain their identity even after they had accepted the rule of black invaders from the north about two hundred years ago. The Venda are pacifists at heart, and they have a saying: *"Mu*ḓ*i wa gozwi a u na malila"* ("In the homestead of the coward there is no weeping"). When their country was later invaded from the south by blacks who were fleeing from the advance of the whites, the Venda preferred to retreat to the safety of their mountains and wait for them to pass. They were unwilling to accept cultural innovations or to incorporate strangers into their political system on terms that were likely to diminish, rather than increase, cooperation and "humanness" (*vhuthu*) in their society. On the other hand, during the latter half of the nineteenth century, the Venda adopted and accepted as "songs of the Venda-speaking people" several foreign songs and styles of music from their neighbors in the north and south.

It may seem surprising that such musical people should have shown little interest in, and comparatively little ability for, the sounds and techniques of European music. The reasons are partly technical, but chiefly political. First, the sort of music that has been disseminated in missions and schools has often been the dullest type of European institutional music, and even the best music has invariably been distorted by the way in which it was taught by the whites. There has been no real contact with the original of the unfamiliar idiom; none of the Europeans who have passed on the tradition have been accomplished musicians, and so both they and the Africans they have trained have often been as unsure about the correct reading of the scores as those they have taught. White "experts" have assured them that sentiment and expression (which often amount to wearing bright uniforms at interschool singing competitions) are more important than accuracy. This is a notion quite foreign to traditional Venda music, in which accuracy is always expected and sentiment generally assumed, but it is one strong enough to have had disastrous results in the process of assimilating European music, and so it is not surprising that the apparently musical Venda have generally failed to excel in performing European music, even when they have wanted to do so.

Political factors were probably even more significant than the technical barriers I have described. Although the gospel and the education the missionaries brought were at first well received by the Venda, the white administration and the commercial exploitation that came in their wake were not. Since 1900 the Venda have not been able to retreat to their mountain fastnesses, as they did with earlier invaders. They have been compelled by superior physical force to put up with an authoritarian system that contradicts traditional African democracy. Is it surprising, therefore, that indifference and even hostility to European music should go along with their resistance to white domination? The general reaction to European music is in keeping with the function of music in their society, and it must be seen as a sociological as well as a musical phenomenon.

Much Venda music is occasional, and its performance is a sign of the activity of social groups. Most adult Venda know what is happening merely by listening to its sounds. During girls' initiation, whenever a novice is being taken down to the river or back to her initiation hut, the women and girls who accompany her warn people of their approach with a special song, in which the lower lip is flapped with the forefinger.

Example 6

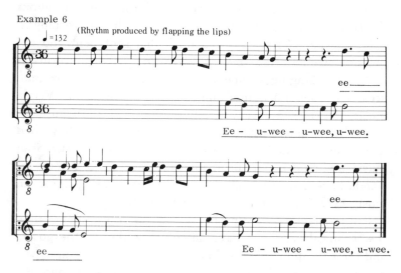

The following song, with its unusual prelude, indicates that a novice is being taken from her home for initiation. The melody will be recognized even by women who cannot hear the words.

Example 7

During the various stages of the girls' schools, instruction is given both directly and indirectly by means of symbolic dances, which are often very strenuous physical exercises, performed to a variety of complex rhythms. One song tells girls not to gossip.

Example 8

The use of left and right hands (which may be reversed) in the drum parts is shown by the direction of the tails of the notes.

The Venda learn to understand the sounds of music as they understand speech. No fewer than sixteen different styles are distinguished, with different rhythms and combinations of singers and instruments; and within these styles are further subdivisions of style, as well as different songs within each division. For example, at the *sungwi* initiation school for girls, there are four main types of song:

1. *Nyimbo dza u sevhetha* (songs for dancing round) are sung by the girls as they dance counterclockwise in a circle round the drums. The tempo of the songs is rapid, and they are sung more often than any other type of song at the school. Classed with them are two songs with special rhythms, a "song of dismissal" (*luimbo lwa u edela*, literally, song for sleeping), which always terminates a session; and a recruiting song (*luimbo lwa u wedza*, literally, song for helping a person across a river), which is sung when senior members go round recruiting.

2. *Nyimbo dza vhahwira* (songs of the masked dancers) are sung when the masked dancers perform in front of the

girls. The tempo varies, with fast and slow episodes to accompany different phases of the dance and distinctive rhythms to mark the various steps.

3. *Nyimbo dza dzingoma* (songs for special rites) accompany certain ordeals that the novices must undergo when they are in the second stage of initiation. Each one has a distinctive rhythmic pattern.

4. *Nyimbo dza milayo* (songs of the laws of the school) are sung by the novices and any graduates present. They kneel on the ground by the drums while *muluvhe*, the girl appointed to be in charge of the novices, leads the singing.

Figure 5 summarizes the different types of communal music recognized by the Venda and indicates the times of year when they may or may not be performed.

Although the Venda generally classify their music according to its social function, and the name for the function and its music is often the same, the criteria of discrimination are formal and musical. It is by its sound, and particularly by its rhythm and the make-up of its vocal and/or instrumental ensemble, that the function of music is recognized. The contexts in which songs are sung are not exclusive, but the way in which they are sung is generally determined by context. Thus, a beer song may be adapted as a play song for the girls' *domba* initiation, in which case a drum accompaniment will be added and the call-response form may be elaborated into a sequence of interlocking melodic phrases. Similarly, a number of different transformations of the national dance, *tshikona*, may be performed on Venda musical instruments. They sound different, but they are all called *tshikona* and are conceived as variations on a theme in the "languages" of the different instruments.

When the Venda discuss or classify different types of song, they generally distinguish between songs that are proper to the function and those which have been adopted and adapted. As I believe that this is a common phenomenon in central

COMMUNAL MUSIC OF THE VENDA

October	November	December	January	February	March	April	May	June	July	August	September
Tshimedzi	Lara	Nyendavhusiku	Phando	Luhuhwi	Thafamuhwe	Lambamai	Shundunthule	Fulwi	Fulwana	Thangule	Khubvumedzi

WORK ———————————————————————→ REST ————→
SCHOOL EXAMS   SCHOOL HOLIDAY   SCHOOL HOLIDAY

SPRING   S U M M E R   A U T U M N   W I N T E R   SPRING
t   s   h   i   l   i   m   o   luṱavula   tshifhetho   Vhuriha or mariha   mavhuya-haya   madzula-haya
THE TIME FOR HOEING   THE TIME OF GOING HOME   THE TIME OF STAYING AT HOME

R A I N S   HEAVY RAINS   NO HERDING
PLANTING   W E E D I N G   FIRST COBS OF GREEN MAIZE zwikoli   REAPING   COLLECTING GROUND-NUTS   ANIMALS GRAZE FREELY ON MAIZE FIELDS

FOR HOEING   FOR WEEDING   FOR THRESHING AND BUILDING HOUSES
WORK SONGS   nyimbo dza davha
1 POUNDING SONGS   maṱhuwe   GIFTS OF BEER mirula
BEER SONGS   malende   FROM WIFE-GIVERS vho-makhulu   TO WIFE-TAKERS vhakwasha

2 CHILDREN'S SONGS   nyimbo dza vhana   STORIES AND SONGS ngano AT HOME / FTER DARK
PLAY DANCES dzombo, nzekenzeke, tshinzerere, tshifhase
OUTDOORS ON MOONLIGHT NIGHTS

3   GIRLS' DANCE WITH DRUMS   tshigombela

4   BOYS' DANCES WITH REED-PIPES [PENTATONIC] AND DRUMS
tshikanganga, givha, visa

5   mabepha MUSICAL EXPEDITIONS   tshikona   tshigombela   tshigombela
FROM TOWN AT EASTER   tshikanganga etc.   tshikona, tshikanganga etc.

6   BOYS' CIRCUMCISION SCHOOL
m u r u n d u

7 GIRLS' CIRCUMCISION SCHOOL   sungwi or musevhetho   TERMS OF ABOUT THREE MONTHS THROUGHOUT YEAR, WITH PERIODS OF REST

8 POSSESSION DANCES   tshele [lit. HAND RATTLE] DANCED INDOORS WHEN SICKNESS IS ngoma dza midzimu, ngoma dza malombo ATTRIBUTED TO SPIRIT'S DESIRE TO ENTER SUFFERER'S BODY [on DRUMS OF THE ANCESTOR SPIRITS etc.] PERFORMED OUTDOORS FOR 4 TO 6 DAYS

9 GIRLS' INITIATION SCHOOL   vhusha   HELD WHEN A GIRL'S PUBERTY IS REPORTED TO HEADMAN, EACH SESSION LASTS 4 DAYS

10   GIRLS' INITIATION SCHOOL   tshikanda
HELD ONLY BEFORE BEGINNING OF domba IN A DISTRICT. LASTS A MONTH

11 BOYS' AND GIRLS' PRE-MARITAL INITIATION SCHOOL   domba
HELD BY CHIEFS AND HEADMEN AT INTERVALS OF ABOUT 5 YEARS IN EACH DISTRICT, AND AFTER ACCESSION OF NEW RULER

12 NATIONAL DANCE WITH REED-PIPES [HEPTATONIC] AND DRUMS   tshikona
FOR INSTALLING, OR COMMEMORATING DEATH OF, A RULER. FOR thevhula SACRIFICIAL RITES AT GRAVES OF RULERS' ANCESTORS FOR ANY IMPORTANT OCCASION

13 MUSIC OF SEPARATIST CHURCHES   nyimbo dza zion

14 MUSIC OF EUROPEAN-RUN CHURCHES   nyimbo dza vhatendi

15 SCHOOL MUSIC   nyimbo dza tshikolo

16 MODERN SECULAR LIGHT MUSIC, JAZZ etc.   nyimbo dza tshikhuwa, dza dzhaivi etc.
FOR WEDDINGS, BIRTHDAY PARTIES, SOCIALS etc.   LEARNT THROUGH URBAN CONTACTS, FROM RECORDS etc.

N.B. THE UNBROKEN LINES INDICATE DAILY, OR AT LEAST REGULAR, PERFORMANCES DURING THE PERIOD MARKED.
THE BROKEN LINES INDICATE IRREGULAR PERFORMANCES.

FIGURE 5. *Diagram showing the different types of communal music recognized by the Venda, and indicating the times of year when they may or may not be performed.*

and southern African music, and one that needs careful investigation by fieldworkers, I will mention a particularly good example that I encountered when working with the Gwembe

Tonga of Zambia. I recorded what was described to me as "a grinding song," and the context left me in little doubt about its function. In a different context, the same melody was described to me as a *mankuntu* dance song for young people, and the new context also left me in little doubt about its function. The only differences between the two performances were in their rhythm, tempo, and social context. The song was not, in fact, a grinding song, but a song sung while grinding. It happened to be a *mankuntu* dance song that was currently popular, and the woman's use of it while grinding was comparable to a performance of "Hark, the Herald Angels Sing!" over the washing-up at Christmas time.

People's classifications of songs by form and by function may provide important evidence of musical and extramusical transformation processes that are acceptable in a culture. They may also be relevant in assessing the effects of music. For example, there is a Venda song about loneliness and death which I heard sung with great gusto at a party, and with no trace of sorrow. On another occasion, I was talking one day to an old, blind master of initiation, and he suddenly began to sing this same song. He was about to stand up and dance when his son stopped him, saying, "Don't dance, old man!" Since his father was singing a sad song, he must be full of sorrow and so there was no point in intensifying the emotion by dancing, especially as there was a risk that he might fall and hurt himself. The son was deeply moved, but when I asked him about the song he replied simply that it was a beer song. He could have described it as a "song of sorrow," but he preferred to give it its formal classification.

The value of music in society and its differential effects on people may be essential factors in the growth or atrophy of musical abilities, and people's interest may be less in the music itself than in its associated social activities. On the other hand, musical ability may never develop without some extramusical motivation. For every infant prodigy whose interest and ability fizzled out because he could not relate his music to life with his fellows, there must be thousands of people who now love music as part of the experience of life and deeply regret that they neglected to practice or were not properly taught an instrument. This conflict has been greatly alleviated by some music education programs, but the combination of social, physical, and musical activity is not as total as in Venda society. When I watched young Venda developing their bodies, their friendships, and their sensitivity in communal dancing, I could not help regretting the hundreds of afternoons I had wasted on the rugby field and in boxing rings. But then I was brought up not to cooperate, but to compete. Even music was offered more as a competitive than as a shared experience.

Although the structure of most Venda music demands a high degree of cooperation for performance, it would be wrong to suggest that all musical and associated social experiences are equally shared. For instance, on the last day of the *tshikanda* girls' initiation, the sullen, silent demeanor of the novices contrasts strongly with the excited singing and dancing of the old ladies in charge and the other graduates present. Even though the girls have to put on a show of humility and detachment, it is hard to believe that they are concealing anything but resignation and indifference to the music they are required to perform. When I asked them about their reactions, I detected a significant difference between the girls' "It's the custom," and the adults' "It's the custom. It's nice!"

Similarly, the exciting rhythms of the Venda possession dance (*ngoma dza midzumi*) do not send every Venda into a trance. They send only members of the cult, and then only when they are dancing at their own homes, with which the spirits of the ancestors who possess them are familiar. The effectiveness of the music depends on the context in which it is both performed and heard. But ultimately it depends on the music, as I found out once when I was playing one of the drums. Dancers take turns coming out into the "arena," and at first there were no complaints about my efforts. Very soon, however, a senior lady began dancing, and she was expected to go into a trance because the music was being played for her cult group. However, after a few minutes she stopped and insisted that another drummer should replace me! She claimed that I was ruining the effect of the music by "hurrying" the tempo—just enough, I suppose, to inhibit the onset of trance.

The way in which the music of the possession dance becomes effective suggests that kinship is as important a factor as the rhythm of music in having effects on people. But it is not blood relationships so much as their social implications that are the decisive factors, and not the music so much as its social environment and the attitudes developed toward it. After all, if the possession dance music has the power to "send" a woman on one occasion, why should it not do so on another? Is it the social situation that inhibits the otherwise powerful effects of the music? Or is the music powerless without the reinforcement of a special set of social circumstances? It is evidence such as this that makes me skeptical of music association tests which have been administered to subjects in artificial and unsocial settings never envisaged by the creators of the music. Under such conditions, the music cannot help being meaningless, or at least its meanings are hopelessly diverse. It also raises another issue: granted that music cannot express anything extramusical unless the experience to which it refers already exists in the mind of the listener, can it communicate anything at all to unprepared or unreceptive minds? Cannot even a powerful rhythm excite an unprepared person? Or are the Venda women unmoved because they are unwilling? I cannot answer this, but my own love of music and my conviction that it is more than learned behavior make me hope that it is the social inhibitions which are powerful and not the music which is powerless.

Let us return to the matter of kinship in the development of musical ability. The Venda may not consider the possibility of unmusical human beings, but they do recognize that some people perform better than others. Judgment is based on the performer's display of technical brilliance and originality, and the vigor and confidence of his execution. Anyone who troubles to perfect his technique is considered to do so because he is deeply committed to music as a means of sharing some experience with his fellows. A sincere desire to express feeling is not accepted as an excuse for inaccurate or incompetent performance, as it often is in the confused world of modern Pop and so-called Folk music. If a person wants to do his thing, he is expected to do it well. The ability of a master drummer *(matsige)* at a possession dance is assessed by the sounds he produces, and not by the extent to which he rolls his eyes and throws his body about.

The Venda may suggest that exceptional musical ability is biologically inherited, but in practice they recognize that social factors play the most important part in realizing or suppressing it. For instance, a boy of noble birth might show great talent, but as he grows up he will be expected to abandon regular musical performance for the more serious (for him) business of government. This would not mean that he would cease to listen critically and intelligently to music: in fact, important guidance to successful government might be given to him in song. Conversely a girl of noble birth has every encouragement to develop her musical capacities, so that as a woman she can play an active role in supervising the girls' initiation schools which are held in the homes of rulers, and for which music is an indispensable adjunct of their didactic and ritual functions. During two months of daily rehearsals of the young girls' dance, *tshigombela*, I watched the young relatives of a headman emerge as outstanding performers, although at first they did not seem to be more musical than their age-mates. I am sure that the key to their development as dancers was the praise and the interest shown in them by the women in the audience, who were mostly from the headman's family, and who therefore knew the girls by name because they were relatives. It was surely the social consequences of blood relationship that affected the growth of their musicality, rather than special, genetically inherited musical capacities. Again, it is not surprising that masters of initiation tend to "inherit" the craft from their fathers. A master must know many songs and rituals, and so his son is in a favored position when he assists his father on the job.

In Venda society, exceptional musical ability is therefore expected of people who are born into certain families or social groups in which musical performance is essential for maintaining their group solidarity. Just as musical performance is the central factor that justifies the continued existence of an orchestra as a social group, so a Venda possession cult group, or a *domba* initiation school, or a *sungwi* girls' school, would disintegrate if there were no music. Only a few of those who are born into the right group actually emerge as exceptional musicians, and what seems to distinguish them from others is that they perform better because they have devoted more time and energy to it. In applauding the mastery of exceptional musicians, the Venda applaud human effort, and in being able to recognize mastery in the musical medium, listeners reveal that their general musical competence is no less than that of the musicians whom they applaud. We should remember that the existence of Bach and Beethoven depends on discriminating audiences as much as on performers, just as some Venda ancestors canot return to their homes except by the good offices of their descendants.

Although communal music dominates the Venda musical scene, and social factors influence the development of musical ability, there is individual music making, and good solo instrumentalists can emerge without any of the incentives I have described. Young growing girls confide in the quiet, intimate tones of a *lugube* musical bow or its modern equivalent, the jaw's harp. Youths sing of the joys and pangs of love while accompanying themselves with an *mbira* or another kind of bow, called *tshihwana*. A third type of bow *(dende)* is most commonly played by semiprofessional musicians who are notoriously popular with women.

The name given to such minstrels—*tshilombe*—is related to words that refer to spirit possession, such as *tshilombo* and *malombo*. The Venda acknowledge that manifestations of musical ability can emerge in unexpected quarters and among unlikely subjects, but insist that they be normalized by logical explanations. The term *tshilombe* should be regarded as not so much an acclamation of genius or of exceptional talent as an occupational description. An outstanding individual musician is one who puts himself in touch with spiritual forces, like a doctor or the member of a possession cult, and so is able to express a wider range of experiences than most people. It may seem paradoxical that his creative abilities should be expressed in the originality and thoughtfulness of the words he composes, rather than in the music. But there is a reason for this to be found in the balance of two basic principles of Venda music.

As I emphasized in the first chapter, Venda music is distinguished from nonmusic by the creation of a special world of time. The chief function of music is to involve people in shared experiences within the framework of their cultural experience. The form the music takes must serve this function, and so in the normal course of events Venda music becomes more musical and less culture-bound whenever possible, and the restrictions of words are abandoned for the freer musical expression of individuals in community. To ensure that the form does not lose its essential function, the process is inverted in the compositions of certain individuals. The function of such compositions is to jolt and expand the consciousness of Venda audiences by both reflecting and contradicting the spirit of the time. They reflect the political interests of the maximum number of people by contradicting the musical tendencies to which those people are accustomed. The same kind of analysis of musical effectiveness might be applied in other contexts: I would not consider it an exaggeration to say that Beethoven achieved his extraordinary musical power by being *anti*musical and shocking the complacency of his contemporary society. His contemporaries may have been more musical in their treatment of melody, for instance, but their kind of conventional musicality was less relevant to contemporary problems although it was a logical consequence of temporary cognitive processes.

To analyze the composition and appreciation of music in terms of its social function and of cognitive processes that may be applied in other fields of human activity does not in any way diminish the importance of the music itself, and it is in line with the common custom of interrelating a series of human activities and calling them The Arts. However, at this early stage of investigation we should be careful not to assume that music is always created by the same processes, or that its processes are specially related to those employed in the other arts. The processes that in one culture are applied to language or music may in another be applied to kinship or economic organization.

It will be useful to distinguish different kinds of musical communication, which might broadly be described as the utilitarian and artistic uses of music in Venda society. It is clear from the way the Venda talk about it that not all music has the same value. All their music grows out of human experiences and has a direct function in social life, but only some of it is regarded as what John Dewey has called "an instrument indispensable to the transformation of man and his world."

As my examples have shown, much Venda music is merely

a signal or sign of social events and no less utilitarian than commercial jingles, radio station identifications, some incidental music, and the hymns or songs that are essentially the "badges" of different social groups. Many songs of initiation are more important as markers of stages in ritual or as reinforcements or mnemonics of lessons than as musical experiences; work songs coordinate and ease labor; and a special group of beer songs can be used to voice complaints and make requests when parties of women take gifts of beer to the homes of their in-laws. As in women's pounding songs, certain children's songs, and songs of protest, a musical framework can ritualize communication in such a way that messages may be conveyed but no counteraction is taken. You do not "go to prison" if you say it in music, and something may be done about your complaint because it may be a warning of growing public feeling.

It is tempting to define the utilitarian functions of Venda music as those in which the effects of music are incidental to the impact of the social situation, and the artistic as those in which the music itself is the crucial factor in the experience. The testimony of the high value attached to *tshikona*, their national dance, and the apparently antimusical performance by acknowledged experts does not contradict this argument when we see that it is the process of music making that is valued as much as, and sometimes more than, the finished product. The value of music is, I believe, to be found in terms of the human experiences involved in its creation. There is a difference between music that is occasional and music that enhances human consciousness, music that is simply for having and music that is for being. I submit that the former may be good craftsmanship, but that the latter is art, no matter how simple or complex it sounds, and no matter under what circumstances it is produced.

The music of *tshikona* expresses the value of the largest social group to which a Venda can really feel he belongs. Its

A trio on the large mbiras (mbila dza madeza).

A boy plays the small mbira (mbila tshipai).

Dende *musical bow.*

A duet on two mouth bows (zwihwana, *singular* tshihwana).

A trio of three-holed transverse flutes
(zwitiringo, *singular* tshi̧tiringo).

Boys' ḑiliṭili *flute, made of an open
tube or river reed with a notched
embouchure and stopped with the
first finger at the distal end.*

The phalaphala *signal horn, made
from the horns of a sable antelope
or kudu.*

Two men play the mbila mtondo *xylophone; a third adds extra notes.*

The dance of the Venda domba *initiation school.*

A Venda team of tshikona *pipe dancers from Johannesburg visits
a rural area during Easter vacation.*

A Venda minstrel (tshilombe) *sings and entertains with puppets at
a beer-drink organized by a rotating credit association*
(tshitokofela) *in a rural area.*

Solo Venda dancer leaping during performance of pentatonic reed-pipe music (tshikanganga or visa). This style of dancing is called u gaya, *as in the second part of* tshigombela, *and is distinguished from the communal dancing (u tshina) in the first part.*

Novices at a Venda domba *initiation, with their hair recently cut, are led in song by the master of initiation, while his assistant directs them to the crossbeam of the council hut, from which they will hang upside down, like bats, as part of a lesson about childbirth. Note the baby on the back of the mother playing the bass drum.*

performance involves the largest number of people, and its music incorporates the largest number of tones in any single piece of Venda music involving more than one or two players. From what I have said about shared experiences in Venda music, it should be clear that *tshikona* is valuable and beautiful to the Venda, not only because of the quantity of people and tones involved, but because of the quality of the relationships that must be established between people and tones whenever it is performed. *Tshikona* music can be produced only when twenty or more men blow differently tuned pipes with a precision that depends on holding one's own part as well as blending with others, and at least four women play different drums in polyrhythmic harmony. Furthermore, *tshikona* is not complete unless the men also perform in unison the different steps which the dance master directs from time to time.

The effectiveness of *tshikona* is not a case of MORE = BETTER. It is an example of the production of the maximum of available human energy in a situation that generates the highest degree of individuality in the largest possible community of individuals. *Tshikona* provides an experience of the best of all possible worlds, and the Venda are fully aware of its value. *Tshikona*, they say, is *lwa-ha-masia-khali-i-tshi-vhila*, "the time when people rush to the scene of the dance and leave their pots to boil over." *Tshikona* "makes sick people feel better, and old men throw away their sticks and dance." *Tshikona* "brings peace to the countryside." Of all shared experiences in Venda society, a performance of *tshikona* is said to be the most highly valued: the dance is connected with ancestor worship and state occasions, incorporates the living and the dead, and is the most universal of Venda music.

It is because music can create a world of virtual time that Gustav Mahler said that it may lead to "the 'other world'— the world in which things are no longer subject to time and space." The Balinese speak of "the other mind" as a state of being that can be reached through dancing and music. They refer to states in which people become keenly aware of the true nature of their being, of the "other self" within themselves and other human beings, and of their relationship with the world around them. Old age, death, grief, thirst, hunger, and other afflictions of this world are seen as transitory events. There is freedom from the restrictions of actual time and complete absorption in the "Timeless Now of the Divine Spirit," the loss of self in being. We often experience greater intensity of living when our normal time values are upset, and appreciate the quality rather than the length of time spent doing something. The virtual time of music may help to generate such experiences.

There is excitement in rhythm and in the progression of organized sound, in the tension and relaxations of harmony or melody, in the cumulative evolution of a fugue, or in the infinite variations on the theme of movement from and back to a tone center. The motion of music alone seems to awaken in our bodies all kinds of responses. And yet people's responses to music cannot be fully explained without some reference to their experiences in the culture of which the notes are signs and symbols. If a piece of music moves a variety of listeners, it is probably not because of its outward form but because of what the form means to each listener in terms of human experience. The same piece of music may move different people in the same sort of way, but for different reasons. You can enjoy a piece of plainchant because you are a Roman Catholic, or because you like the sound of the music: you need not have a "good ear" to enjoy it as a Catholic, nor need you be a believer to enjoy it as music. In both cases the enjoyment depends on a background of human experience.

Even if a person describes musical experiences in the technical language of music, he is in fact describing emotional experiences which he has learned to associate with particular patterns of sound. If another person describes his experience in the same musical tradition, he may be describing a similar, if not identical, emotional experience. Musical terminology can be a language with which to describe human emotional experience, just as membership in the Venda possession cult offers both a certain type of experience and a way of talking about it. Thus, under certain conditions, the sound of music may recall a state of consciousness that has been acquired through processes of social experience. Whether the effective agent is the right social situation, as in the Venda possession cult, or the right musical situation, as in the responses of two similarly trained musicians, it is effective only because of associations between certain individual and cultural experiences.

I am sure that many of the functions of music in Venda society which I have described will recall to you similar situations in other societies. My general argument has been that, if the value of music in society and culture is to be assessed, it must be described in terms of the attitudes and cognitive processes involved in its creation, and the functions and effects of the musical product in society. It follows from this that there should be close structural relationships among the function, content, and form of music. Robert Kauffman has drawn my attention to a passage in LeRoi Jones's *Blues People* (New York: William Morrow, 1963), in which he says that the basic hypothesis of his book depends on understanding that "music can be seen to be the result of certain attitudes, certain specific ways of thinking about the world, and only ultimately about the 'ways' in which music can be made" (p. 153). It is enough that this should be said and accepted. But I think it is useful if the argument can be reinforced with demonstrations of how it works out in practice. This is something that ethnomusicologists can do, and most of my work during the past fifteen years has been directed toward the discovery of structural relationships between music and social life.

Culture and Society in Music

$\mathcal{M}$USIC can express social attitudes and cognitive processes, but it is useful and effective only when it is heard by the prepared and receptive ears of people who have shared, or can share in some way, the cultural and individual experiences of its creators.

Music, therefore, confirms what is already present in society and culture, and it adds nothing new except patterns of sound. But it is not a luxury, a spare-time activity to be sandwiched between sports and art in the headmaster's report. Even if I believed that music was, or should be, merely a means of decorating social events, I would still have to explain how the music of many composers can excite me although the cavortings of their patrons are a bore. When E. M. Forster said, "History develops, art stands still," he was referring to their subject matter, to the fact that history is about events but art is about feelings. That is why we can also say that history dies but art lives, although art is a reflection of history. I share the Venda view that music is essential for the very survival of man's humanity, and I found it significant that as a subject for discussion they generally greeted music more enthusiastically and with more erudition than history, though not less than current politics. This may have been partly a response to my own bias, but I think it also reflected the Venda concern for life as a process of becoming, rather than as a stage in evolutionary progress.

We shall do well to look at music in the same way. And so, before I work back to the surface patterns of music from the cultural and social processes to which I have reduced them, before I discuss the origins of music in culture and society, I want to dispose of two kinds of evolutionary approach to music history which are of no use in seeking an answer to the question, How musical is man? They are useless chiefly because they can never be proved. The first approach seeks to understand the meaning and forms of music by speculating about its historical origins in bird song, mating calls, and a host of other reactions of some mythical "primitive" man to his environment. Since the chief sources of information for this guesswork have been, and can only be, the musical practices of living people, and a knowledge of music's origins is useful only for understanding these practices better, the exercise is clearly futile.

The second kind of evolutionary approach is concerned with the development of musical styles as things in themselves. It tends to assume that there is a world history of music, in which man began by using one or two tones and then gradually discovered more and more tones and patterns of sound. It leads to such statements as: "In the growth of great civilizations, music is the first of the arts to emerge and the last to develop." Such remarks usually ignore the fact that our knowledge of past music is often limited to what literate classes chose to recognize or record of such activities. Some white missionaries in the Sibasa district, for instance, were astonished that it could take more than six months to learn all there was to know about Venda music because their ears were closed to the variety and complexity of its sounds.

The absence of information on music in the records of the

elite does not mean that there was no good music in the lives of ordinary people; nor is the apparent simplicity of some contemporary musical styles evidence that their music is a survival from a stage in the history of world music. In 1885, Alexander John Ellis, the man who is generally regarded as the father of ethnomusicology, demonstrated that musical scales are not natural but highly artificial, and that laws of acoustics may be irrelevant in the human organization of sound. In spite of his timely warning, there are still some ethnomusicologists who write as if it were their task to fill in the gaps of musical history by describing the musical styles of exotic cultures. Even if they do not say it in so many words, their techniques of analysis betray affection for an evolutionary view of music. Musical styles cannot be heard as stages in the evolution of music, as judged in terms of one particular civilization's concepts of music. Each style has its own history, and its present state represents only one stage in its own development; this may have followed a separate and unique course, although its surface patterns may suggest contacts with other styles. Moreover, even though people are sometimes more conservative about music than about other aspects of culture, it is hard to believe that in some parts of the world there has been no musical innovation for thousands of years.

Speculative histories of world music are a complete waste of effort. Even if we knew how musical styles had changed in the cultures which are cited as evidence of stages in the development of music, the knowledge would be of only encyclopedic interest. It would give us little or no insight into human creativity in music unless we had corresponding evidence on the cultural and social environment in which the musical developments took place. On the other hand, if cultural and social history is well documented, studies of music history are both possible and useful. There is a vast difference between studies such as Paul Henry Lang's *Music in Western*

Civilization, Hugo Leichtentritt's *Music, History and Ideas,* and Alec Harman's and Wilfrid Mellers' volumes on *Man and His Music,* in which the origins of certain aspects of musical style are sought in the social movements and philosophical conventions of the time, and studies that trace musical development in terms of more tones to the octave, more thirds to the chord, and more instruments to the orchestra.

Where, for instance, would our speculative music historian place the Venda in his history of world music? There are *mbiras* that have five-, six-, or seven-tone scales, and sets of reed pipes that use either five- or seven-tone scales. The melodies of songs may use anything from one to seven tones, selected from various heptatonic modes. Songs that use five tones may be based on a pentatonic scale or on selections of five tones from a heptatonic mode (like the "Ode to Joy" in Beethoven's Ninth Symphony!). If our music historian gives the Venda the credit of producing the heptatonic scale themselves and does not assume that they must have borrowed it from a "higher" culture, I suspect that he might describe their music as being in a stage of transition from pentatonic to heptatonic music—a fascinating example of musical evolution in action! The only trouble about such a description is that social and cultural evidence contradicts it. For example, the Venda used a heptatonic xylophone and heptatonic reed pipes long before they adopted the pentatonic reed pipes of their southern neighbors, the Pedi, who in turn say that they adopted and adapted the heptatonic reed pipe music of the Venda. According to evolutionary theories of music history, the Venda should be going backward—like the Chinese, who selected a pentatonic scale for their music although they knew and had used "bigger and better" scales!

It may be argued that I have used one kind of speculative history in order to throw out another, and that the stated cultural origins of Venda and Pedi music may be no less ethnocentric and inaccurate, as rationalizations of a system, than a concept of musical evolution that explains patterns of sound in a different way. To this objection I would reply that in studying musical systems I am primarily concerned with historical *relevance*. Even if we knew exactly how the Venda got *tshikona, domba,* and a heptatonic scale (and I doubt if we shall ever know), and even if it were true that the heptatonic music had evolved from the pentatonic, it would not contribute much to our understanding of the Venda musical system or of the development of musicality in Venda society. I am interested in Venda music more as the product of human minds in Venda culture and society than as a stage in the history of world music.

In asking how musical is man, I am obviously concerned with all aspects of the origins of music, but not with speculative origins, or even with origins which a foreign historian thinks he can detect, but which are not recognized by the creators of the music. The origins of music that concern me are those which are to be found in the psychology and in the cultural and social environment of its creators, in the assembly of processes that generate the patterns of sound. If music expresses attitudes, we should expect correlations between the different attitudes and the patterns of sound with which they are expressed.

To what extent is music a "language of emotions, akin to speech," as Deryck Cooke has claimed in *The Language of Music*? The thesis must be considered in the context in which it is proposed: European tonal music between 1400 and 1953. Cooke has shown that specific musical figures seeem to be used again and again to convey similar feelings, and that the use of this kind of code is an essential feature of musical communication. His argument goes a long way toward bridging the gap between formal and expressive analyses of music, and toward showing exactly how music can be described as the expression of certain attitudes. For instance, he describes the descending progression 5-(4)-3-(2)-1 (MINOR) as a figure "which has been much used to express an 'incoming' painful emotion, in a context of finality: acceptance of, or yielding to grief; discouragement and depression; passive suffering; and the despair connected with death" (p. 133). Thus he compares a phrase of Gibbons' madrigal "What Is Our Life?" with the opening of the finale of Tchaikovsky's *Pathetique* Symphony:

Example 9

Cooke's thesis impressed me at first because it seemed to make sense in terms of my own musical experience. For instance, I had noticed and felt the musical and expressive similarity between the pleading melody in the "Recordare Jesu Pie" of Benjamin Britten's *War Requiem* (see Example 10) and the figure with which Mahler accompanies the nostalgic words, "Ich sehne mich, O Freund, am deiner Seite die Schoenheit dieses Abends zu geniessen," in "Der Abscheid," the last song of *Das Lied von der Erde* (Universal Edition, sections 23, 30, and 63 to the end) (see Example 11). The figure 1-3-4-5 (MINOR) also opens the spiritual, "Nobody Knows the Trouble I See" (see Example 12). Same figure, same kind of feeling. Deryck Cooke quotes other instances of this figure and describes it as "an assertion of sorrow, a complaint, a protest against misfortune" (*Language of Music*, p. 122).

Example 10

Example 11

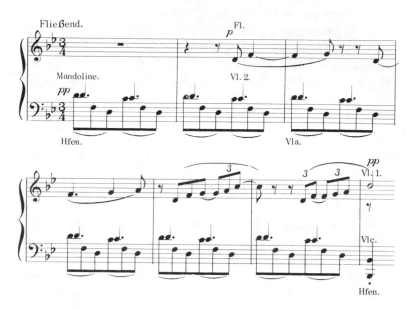

Example 12

No-bod-y knows the trou-ble I see, Lord, No-bod-y knows the trou-ble I see.

Again, although I have deliberately never read any analyses of Mahler's Ninth and Tenth symphonies because I first want to find out what the music says to *me*, I react quite definitely to two parallel sequences of intervals in their final movements (in the case of the Tenth, I refer to Deryck Cooke's performing version). First, in the twenty-third bar of the last movement of the Ninth, the first violins play the tones of a *descending* scale, but in *rising* pairs of falling tones.

Example 13

Then in the Tenth, there is an *ascending* scale which is played in *descending* groups of rising tones (bar 327 of the last movement).

Example 14

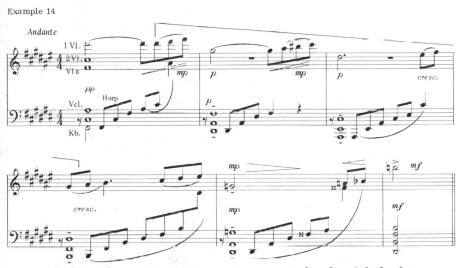

I will make no attempt to express in words what I feel when I hear this music, because Mahler explicitly stated that he felt the need to express himself in music only when "indefinable emotions make themselves felt," and if they could have been expressed in language he would have done so. I will merely say that for me they express something about life and death and man's struggle for fulfillment and spiritual peace. The final chords of the Tenth seem to express ultimate resignation—whether they were written by Mahler or by Deryck Cooke!

Now, have I received the attitudes that prompted Mahler to compose those notes, or have I reinterpreted them in the light of my own experience? And does anyone else feel about them in the same way? Am I out on a limb, like the novices in the *tshikanda* girl's initiation, listening to Mahler but not hearing him? *Can* anyone else hear those notes as I do, or as Mahler did? Is the purpose of musical experience to be alone in company? Is there no hope of establishing common rela- tionships through music except where there is a fairly specific extramusical program? Could "soul" music affect Black Americans if its forms were not associated with a whole set of extramusical experiences which Black Americans share? In spite of the beautifully stated antiwar message of Britten's *War Requiem*, can all those who share his sentiments share the intense message of his music? Does it really mean the same to the Russian, English, and German solo singers who made the first recording of the work? To those who share aspects of Britten's cultural, social, and musical background, the music may enhance the pity of Wilfred Owen's poetry and create a greater horror of war than could the poetry on its own. For others, the poetry may be a stirring experience, but the music a bore. We cannot say that they share the experi- ence of the poetry more than that of the music, because they, like Britten and most of his listeners, did not share Owen's ultimately fatal experience of trench warfare. We can only say that they share the experience of the convention of the poetry more easily than the convention of the music.

Although "'music can reveal the nature of feelings with a detail and truth that language cannot approach" (to quote Susanne Langer, *Philosophy in a New Key* [New York: Men- tor Books, 1948], p. 191), it is also tied to the culture in a way in which the descriptive capacities of language are not. Con- sider the elements of British and European culture in the

music of Britten's *War Requiem*—and, again, in this description I shall speak of the work as it strikes me: I have not
read any commentaries on it. The very first two bars of the
work set the stage for death, with the tolling of a bell and the
intoning of the opening words of the Requiem Mass.

Example 15

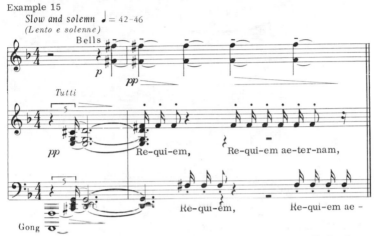

Later, the sounds of boys' voices and an organ recall the hope
and innocence of childhood,

Example 16

and brass instruments and bugle-call motifs recall warfare.

Example 17

Musical imitations of the sounds of shrapnel accompany the words of Owen's jaunty soldiers singing, "Out there we've walked quite friendly up to Death." Now it is the shrapnel that sings aloft, but a few moments before, in the "Rex tremendae, majestatis," it was heaven. The military associations of drums are reinforced when they are used to refer to the firing of artillery.

Example 18

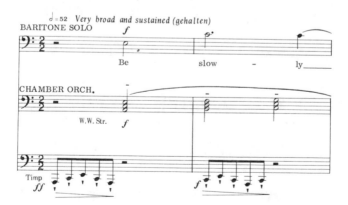

But drums and trumpets may also take us to heaven and divine judgment in the "Dies Irae," and Britten makes a powerful contrast between "Tuba mirum spargens sonum" and "Bugles sang, saddening the evening air"—

Example 19

Example 20

the glorious trumpets of God, and then the bloody bugles of man!

To someone who has been immersed in the culture of the composer, the sounds Britten uses and the contrasts he makes between them can be heart-rending and poignant. For one whose school friends have been killed in action, it has the same kind of effect as the contrasting photographs of cricket fields, choirboys, rockets, and war which Peter Brook showed at the beginning of his film of *Lord of the Flies*. In this case, my reactions to the music may be closer to the feelings Britten had when he wrote it than they were in the case of Mahler's Ninth and Tenth symphonies. But have Britten and Mahler really used a language that is in any way akin to speech?

Composers acquire characteristics of style by listening to the music of the past and present. Britten acknowledges a debt to Mahler, and both Britten and Mahler spent some time in the United States. But is there really a common factor in their use of the same figure in the *War Requiem* and *Das Lied von der Erde*? And is it likely that the creators of "Nobody Knows" would have used the same musical language as Britten and Mahler, when it is clear (to me, at any rate) that spirituals are a development of African principles of music making rather than an imitation of the European? (For instance, the basic meter of "Nobody Knows" is 3+3+2, and the apparently un-African melody may have begun as the lower part of a characteristically African "falling" melody, which was given the harmonic treatment that is typical of African music and not necessarily borrowed from Europe.)

Just as Britten assigns different meanings to the same timbre in the context of a single work, so the same pattern of melody may have a variety of expressive meanings, and in fact it is this variety in the context of unity which may add to the expressive power of music. In Vivaldi's *The Four Seasons* (Op. 8), similar scales and arpeggios depict different subjects ranging from the staggering of drunken peasants in "Autumn" to icy winds in "Winter." Even without a knowledge of the sonnets that inspired the music, the meanings of the similar musical figures are clearly different when heard in the context of the work. Again, the marchlike melodies of Mahler's Third and Sixth symphonies, and the March in Act 1, scene 3 of Berg's *Wozzeck*, when Marie is admiring the sergeant-major, have nothing to do with feelings about war. Their musical and dramatic contexts suggest entirely different meanings.

None of these musical meanings is absolute even within the same European musical tradition, in which the rules are clearly stated and the system of learning them has been similar for centuries. They depend not only on the context of the work, but also on the musical conventions of the time. Much has been written about the use of musical figures to illustrate ideas, especially in the music of J. S. Bach. But the music of Bach and Handel cannot be fully understood without reference to the eighteenth-century view of the world, in which aesthetic theories included "a complicated doctrine of emotional expression going back to certain correlations of rhythm and melodic line with various emotions" (Hugo Leichtentritt, *Music, History and Ideas* [Cambridge, Mass.; Harvard University Press, 1946], p. 142). For instance, F major was the key of the pastoral idyll, and F-sharp major was a transcendental key: "Handel's entire harmonic system and style of modulations is based on the underlying meaning of the various keys" (ibid., p. 154). Similarly, if northern Indian music claims to be able to bring out "a nuance of sadness, or of love . . . by careful and impermanent use of the intervals that correspond with these emotions" (Alain Daniélou, *Northern Indian Music* [London: Halcyon Press, 1954], 2:9), it is because the music is heard and performed in the context of Hindu culture and of a musical system that is intricately related to it.

The musical conventions of the eighteenth century stand between the Gibbons madrigal and the Tchaikovsky symphony to which I referred earlier. And so I find it hard to accept that there has been a continuous musical tradition between England in 1612 and Russia in 1893, in which certain musical figures have had corresponding emotional connotations. The only justification for such an argument would be that the emotional significance of certain intervals arises from fundamental features of human physiology and psychology. If this is so, some relationships between musical intervals and human feelings ought to be universal. An example from Africa will be sufficient to question such a theory. It is not sufficient to dismiss the theory altogether, because it is possible that Venda musical conventions have suppressed an innate desire in Venda people to express their emotions in a specific, universal way.

Figure 6a shows a Venda children's song in which small variations in the melody are generated by changes of speech tone. When I first learned to sing it, the Venda told me that I was doing well, but that I sang like a Tsonga (their neighbors to the south). I sang all word phrases to the melody of the first, and I thought that my fault lay in the pitch of my intervals. Eventually, when I realized that the melody should vary, they accepted my performance as truly Venda even if I deliberately sang out of tune. The pattern of intervals is considered more important than their exact pitch, because in certain parts of a melody they are expected to reflect changes in speech tone. Figure 6b shows a children's song in which the speech-tone patterns of the first phrase generate the basic melody, and subsequent variations in words bring about rhythmic, as well as melodic, variations. Such rhythmic changes are sometimes called agogic accents in orthodox musical analysis. Variations in melody and rhythm may therefore indicate not musical preferences, but the incidental consequences of changes in speech tone, which are themselves generated by the use of different words whose sequence is generated by the "story" of the song.

Essential generative factors in the music of these and other Venda songs are therefore extramusical. Parts of the melodies are formal representations of patterns of speech tone, which are also formal and not necessarily related to the meaning and expressive purpose of the words. Relationships between the specific emotional content of the words and the shape of its associated melody may exist, but they would be coincidental.

á = high speech tone   ā = secondary high
â = falling high   à = low
+ = points where some might clap to the melody

FIGURE 6. *Parts of two Venda children's songs, illustrating some effects of changing speech tones on the patterns of melody.*

    This does not mean that the Venda are unmoved by music, or that they regard it as a mere extension of language. The treatment of a girls' *tshigombela* dance song illustrates this very clearly. The tendency is for the music to become more musical as the performance proceeds. Even in solo vocal music like the children's songs, the form of melodies can be divided into call and response sections, reflecting a social situation in which someone "sows" (*-sima*) a song, and others "thunder in response"(*-bvumela*)—a metaphor derived from horticulture. It is only in the call section of the songs that melodies follow the speech-tone patterns of words, and also the general rule that each syllable of a word may be accompanied by only one tone. If performers substitute for words various combinations of phonemes such as *ee, ahee, huwelele wee, yowee,* and so forth, they give themselve greater freedom of musical expression. This is important, because it is the part of the shared experience of musical activity which may become transcendental in its effect on individuals. In the development of a *tshigombela* song during a performance that may last from ten to more than thirty minutes, the straightforward call and response is elaborated into a quasi-contrapuntal sequence, and words are abandoned. During the course of freer musical expression, a variety of melodies come out "on top" because in the excitement of the dance the pitch of the girls' voices rises, and when they cannot reach a tone they transpose it down a fifth or an octave. Thus, falling intervals may sometimes express the feeling, "I can't reach the next tone"!

There are also relationships between variations in the social and emotional content of a *tshigombela* dance and the form of the music, so that a formal analysis of different performances is also an expressive analysis. But unless the formal analysis begins as an analysis of the social situation that generates the music, it is meaningless. One has only to listen to performances on an afternoon when the girls are few in number and bored, and on another occasion when there is a good turnout, an appreciative audience, and an atmosphere of excitement and concern, to realize how and why two performances of the same song can be entirely different in expressive power and in form. The number and quality of variations in rhythm depend on the ability of the drummers and dancers, but it is not simply a matter of running through the gamut of standard patterns which they know. When and how these variations are introduced is what gives the music its expressive power; and this depends on the commitment of those present and the quality of the shared experience that comes into being among performers, and between performers and audience.

I introduced Deryck Cooke's theory of the language of

music because, although I cannot accept it, it is undeniably thought-provoking. I have concluded my criticism with examples from Venda music in order to show why an ethnomusicological approach is necessary even in the study of European music between 1400 and 1953. Cooke cannot be faulted for choosing a particular area of music, but, because his theory is not general enough to apply to *any* culture or society, it is automatically inadequate for European music. It is not sufficiently context-sensitive. Tonal music between 1400 and 1953 cannot be isolated as a thing in itself, especially if it is to be related to human emotions. The aesthetic conventions of the eighteenth century cannot be considered apart from the experience of the social groups who were or were not involved in them. If music serves as a sign or symbol of different kinds of human experience, its performance may help to channel the feelings of listeners in certain directions. A composer who hopes to communicate anything more than pretty sounds must be aware of the associations that different sounds conjure up in the minds of different social groups. It is not simply a matter of expressing feeling by relating sounds in the context of a single piece of music, as in Britten's *War Requiem*. The principles of musical organization must be related to social experiences, of which listening to and performing music form one aspect. The minuet is not simply a musical form borrowed from dancing: it has entirely different social and emotional associations before and after the French Revolution.

From a distance, the forms, techniques, and building materials of music may seem to be cumulative, like a technological tradition. But music is not a branch of technology, though it is affected by technological developments. It is more like philosophy, which may also give a superficial impression of being evolutionary. Each apparently new idea in music, like a new idea in philosophy, does not really grow out of previously expressed ideas, though it may well be limited by them. It is a new emphasis which grows out of a composer's experience of his environment, a realization of certain aspects of the experiences common to all human beings which seem to him to be particularly relevant in the light of contemporary events and personal experiences.

The most important thing about a cultural tradition at any time in its history is the way in which its human components relate to each other. It is in the context of these relationships that emotional experiences are had and shared. Artistic enjoyment is "based essentially upon the reaction of our minds to form" (Franz Boas, *Primitive Art* [New York: Dover, 1955 (1927)], p. 349); but the forms are produced by human minds whose working habits are, I believe, a synthesis of given, universal systems of operation and acquired, cultural patterns of expression. Since these patterns are always acquired through and in the context of social relationships and their associated emotions, the decisive style-forming factor in any attempt to express feeling in music must be its social content. If we want to find the basic organizing principles that affect the shapes of patterns of music, we must look beyond the cultural conventions of any century or society to the social situations in which they are applied and to which they refer.

The selection and use of scales may be the product of social and cultural processes that are not necessarily related to the acoustical properties of sound. In Venda, the use of pentatonic, hexatonic, and heptatonic scales reflects a process of *social* change, in which different groups, with different musical styles, have become incorporated into a larger society. It is strange that even a sociologist should ignore similar social processes in the development of the European tonal system. In his study of *The Rational and Social Foundations of Music* (trans. and ed. Don Martindale, Johannes Riedel, and Gertrude Neuwirth [Carbondale, Ill.: Southern Illinois University Press, 1958]), Max Weber claimed that the European musical system was rationalized from within the tone system: it was

concerned not with real distances on instruments, such as
equidistance between frets or flute holes, but with harmonic
distances. "The appearance of theories dealing with the dis-
sonances marks the beginning of the special musical development of the Occident" (p. 75), because "dissonance is the
basic element of chordal music, motivating the progression
from chord to chord" (p. 6). Weber attributes this development to the scientific attitude that emerged at the time of the
Renaissance. Although he acknowledges that theory follows
practice and that "modern chordal harmony belonged to prac-
tical music long before Rameau and the encyclopaedists provided it with a theoretic basis" (p. 103), he does not go
further and show how harmonic music arose out of polyphony, and that polyphony was at first modal and distinguished from monody more by its rhythm than by its tonal
relationships.

The polyphony of early European music is in principle not
unlike the polyrhythm of much African music; in both cases,
performance depends on a number of people holding separate
parts within a framework of metric unity, but the principle is
applied "vertically" to melodies in polyphony, and "horizon-
tally" to rhythmic figures in polyrhythm. The source of both
techniques is surely in cultural concepts and social activity,
such as dancing. The change in European musical technique
from the monody of plainchant to polyphony depended on
mensuration, on the strict organization of rhythm so that
the different singing parts would fit. And mensuration is the
chief feature of dance music, which was a vital activity of
the peasants. The medieval church had allowed only plainchant, which was intended to express the unity of society
within the framework of a church dedicated to God; its style
was completely divorced from the regular rhythms of secular
dancing and the unsophisticated "tonic-dominant" relationships that occur in lively pieces such as "Sumer is icumen
in." It is not surprising that the early masters of polyphony

came from the Netherlands and England, where the peasants had become free during the thirteenth and fourteenth centries, respectively. As the peasants' political importance grew, so their dance music became incorporated in the music written for the church by professional composers.

It is possible that the predominance of thirds and sixths in the music of John Dunstable, and of fourths in the music of the Flemish composers, may be explained as a legacy from the popular music of their societies. (In Africa today, societies who sing in parallel motion show preferences for certain intervals.) Again, the remarkable development of polyphonic music in England during the sixteenth century may have been stimulated as much by the advent of Welsh monarchs and their followers as by the musical invention of individual composers in the first half of the fifteenth century. When the Tudor King Henry VII came to the throne in 1485, he reestablished Welsh influence in England; and Welsh popular music had been noted for its polyphonic technique since at least the twelfth century.

A composer's style is "dictated by the kind of human beings and human emotions" he "tries to bring into his art, using the language elements of his time," says Sidney Finkelstein in *Art and Society* ([New York: International Publishers, 1947], p. 29). The influence of popular culture is strong in the works of many great composers, who have striven to express themselves, and hence their society, in the broadest terms. Lutheran chorales were deliberately derived from "folk songs," and Bach organized much of his music round them. Haydn, Mozart, and Schubert, in particular, organized their music round the Austrian "folk" idiom. Bartók, Kodály, Janáček, Copland, and numerous other composers of national schools have found the greatest stimulus in the sounds of their own societies. In the third and fourth volumes of *Man and His Music,* and especially in *The Sonata Principle (from c. 1750)* (London: Rockliff, 1957), Wilfrid

Mellers has shown how dance forms, the tone and stress of the composer's own language, and particularly the melodies of "folk" music, have all played as vital a part in the process of assimilation and creation as have conventions of musical style. He has drawn attention to the successive dominance of vocal and instrumental forms in the development of techniques of European "art" music, and has linked these developments with changes in the social order (Wilfrid Mellers, *Music and Society* [London: Dobson, 1950], pp. 81, 132). Curt Sachs has likewise discussed the influence of societies' styles of dancing on their melodies (in *World History of the Dance* [New York: W. W. Norton, 1937], pp. 181-203).

Changes in musical style have generally been reflections of changes in society. For example, after about A.D. 1200 in Europe, knights and other secular powers turned increasingly "to the people, whose popular style of singing they adapted to their more refined taste" (Leichtentritt, *Music, History and Ideas*, p. 60). In turning away from the social dominance of the church, they also rejected its music. Similarly, the various styles of Venda music reflect the variety of its social groups and the degree of their assimilation into the body politic. Musical performances are audible and visible signs of social and political groupings in Venda society, and Figure 7 shows their pattern in the social structure. Music in the traditional style is contained in concentric circles symbolic of Venda houses and dance patterns, and nontraditional music is in rectangles, similar to the European house designs that many educated people have adopted. The initiation schools *vhusha*, *tshikanda*, and *domba* are directly controlled by rulers, while *murundu* and *sungwi* are privately owned, but under the auspices of rulers and traditionally oriented. Together with the possession dances (*ngoma dza midzimu*), which are held by family cult groups with the permission of rulers, each of these institutions is regarded very seriously and called *ngoma* (literally, drum). Other types of music may be referred to as

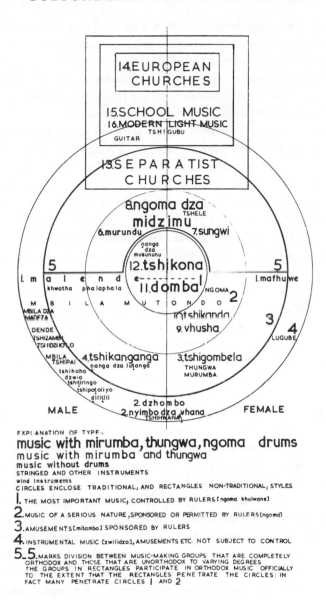

EXPLANATION OF TYPE:-

music with mirumba, thungwa, ngoma   drums
music with mirumba and thungwa
music without drums
STRINGED AND OTHER INSTRUMENTS
wind Instruments
CIRCLES ENCLOSE TRADITIONAL, AND RECTANGLES NON-TRADITIONAL, STYLES

1. THE MOST IMPORTANT MUSIC, CONTROLLED BY RULERS [ngoma khulwane]

2. MUSIC OF A SERIOUS NATURE, SPONSORED OR PERMITTED BY RULERS [ngoma]

3. AMUSEMENTS [mitambo] SPONSORED BY RULERS

4. INSTRUMENTAL MUSIC [zwilidzo], AMUSEMENTS ETC. NOT SUBJECT TO CONTROL

5.-5. MARKS DIVISION BETWEEN MUSIC-MAKING GROUPS THAT ARE COMPLETELY
ORTHODOX AND THOSE THAT ARE UNORTHODOX TO VARYING DEGREES
THE GROUPS IN RECTANGLES PARTICIPATE IN ORTHODOX MUSIC OFFICIALLY
TO THE EXTENT THAT THE RECTANGLES PENETRATE THE CIRCLES: IN
FACT MANY PENETRATE CIRCLES **1** AND **2**

FIGURE 7. *Diagram showing the relationships between musical and
social structure in Venda society. Compare with Figure 5.*

amusements (*mitambo*), but this does not mean they are not an important part of Venda social and political life. The European-run churches came and set themselves up in total opposition to traditional Venda life, but schools and separatist churches have developed music that reflects the syncretism of their social life.

The variety and vigor of Venda musical styles are the product of a political situation similar to that in Austria in the late eighteenth century, when prominent families and princes "rivalled each other in the excellence of their private orchestras" (ibid., p. 173). The diversity of musical styles reflects a diversity that underlies the apparent homogeneity of Venda culture and society, and hence both the historical process that has brought them about, and their meaning in contemporary life. There are only two types of politically regulated communal music that can really bring traditionally oriented Venda together. They are *tshikona*, the national dance, and *domba*, the premarital initiation dance, which used to be performed by youths and girls but is now performed almost exclusively by girls because migrant labor and the growth of school education have changed the pattern of Venda rural life.

The music and dance of the *domba* initiation school provide an astonishing illustration of the way in which formal and expressive elements may be combined to portray symbolically in music the essential themes of a culture. What makes them all the more remarkable is that the process of creation was almost certainly not self-conscious, but the forms are systematically related to their expressive purpose. The Venda explain that *domba* has been with them for centuries, and they have much to say on the functions of the initiation school and the beauty and value of the chief ritual dance. They make no comment on the form of the dance and its music, except to say that "*domba* is *domba*; it's an important rite (*ngoma*)." And yet the music and dance depict an essen-

tial feature of adult life, and their regular performance symbolize the importance of marriage, childbirth, and institutionalized motherhood.

On the surface, *domba* sounds like a regular piece of Venda
music in call-response form, with polyrhythmic accompaniment and musical development of the response. The circular
form of the dance is characteristically Venda, and with a lot
of girls in relatively small dancing grounds, it is not unreas-
onable that they should hold each other. The movement has
been wrongly called "The Python Dance" in illustrated journals and tourist brochures, in which it is cited as one of the
most interesting things about the Venda—presumably because it is performed by a chain of almost naked maidens.
And yet the dance movement, the kind of musical development which the response is given, and the signals for the
beginning and the end of the dance movements are all generated by the expressive functions of the music. What is
more, I could never have discovered this if I had not attended
scores of performances of the dance in different parts of Venda, recorded hundreds of the word-phrases sung by the soloist, noted the relationships among words, dance, and music,
and learned the esoteric symbolism of the school. I had to
immerse myself in Venda culture and society in order to
understand this product of Venda minds.

The analysis of *domba* I present is derived from a combination of different kinds of ethnographic information. I do not
claim that it is the last word on the subject, but at least it is
logical and it arises out of the ethnography. When I began
the analysis, I had no idea how it would turn out, and I never
suspected that the formal and expressive elements would be
so unified. My conclusions were thrust on me by the regulari-
ties and correspondences that emerged from the material I
had collected in the field.

Domba is the last of a series of initiation schools that
prepare girls for marriage. Although there is much emphasis

on sex and reproduction, the schools are not concerned solely with fertility. They are designed to prepare girls for institutionalized motherhood, together with all the rights and obligations that go with it. There is evidence that the content and form of the school have changed over the years, particularly since its "nationalization" by the ancestors of the ruling clans. In the past, when *domba* was a ritual of the commoner clans, the emphasis on physical growth seems to have been stronger. The ruling clans have expanded the political significance of the initiation schools, but the basically physical orientation of the music and dance remains.

Each performance of the dance symbolizes sexual intercourse, and successive performances symbolize the building up of the fetus, for which regular intercourse is thought to be necessary. The music and the dance are not meant to be sexy: they symbolize the mystical act of sexual communion, conception, the growth of the fetus, and childbirth. After three warning drumbeats, the voice of the male soloist, the master of initiation, "pierces the air like an arrow," like a phallus, and the girls reply with a low, murmuring response. The man's voice begins on what is functionally similar to a dominant in Venda tonality, and the girls' voices take the response to the "tonic," the point of relaxation. Three differently pitched drums enter in polyrhythm, two against three, and the song is under way.

The girls are being symbolically roused. After a few repeats of the basic melody, the master sings "the river reed unwinds," and the girls, who are in a line holding each other's bodies, begin to step around the drums. The river reed and the line of girls are both phallic symbols, and the beginning of the dance movement symbolizes the entry of the phallus. The girls immediately begin quasi-orgastic singing which they call *khulo*. As in the *tshikona* national dance, hocket technique is employed. After several minutes, when the master sings the word-phrase *"gudu* has stirred up your entrails," the girls stop moving and lean over toward the center of the dancing circle, symbolizing detumescence.

There is a fire in the center of the dancing place, which must be kept alight throughout the duration of the school.

Example 21

"muffled" beat on center of skin with left hand

"clear" beat on edge of skin with right hand

beat with stick on wooden edge of drum

indicates notes that are yodeled

Example 21 (continued)

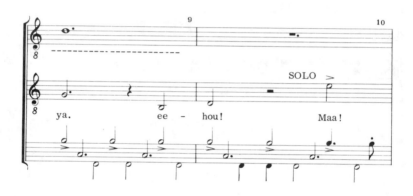

Example 21 (continued)

Example 21 (continued)

DANCE STEPS OF NOVICES

Alternative pattern of basic melody:

STEPS OF MIDABE (Graduates)

The "white" ashes symbolize the semen that is considered necessary for the growth of the fetus. The swinging bass drum is called "the head of the child" in the esoteric symbolism of the school. At the beginning of *domba,* it lies on the ground. After three or four months (though sometimes less, it seems), there is a ceremony at which the drum is "cooked" and then hung from the crossbar. This is like the moving of the child in the womb, symbolized by the dance circle. The symbolism is not conclusive about the drums, but it seems that their different beats express the heartbeats of father, mother, and fetus.

On the last night of the initiation school, the girls dance with their hands above their heads, symbolizing the pains of childbirth and a night of labor. On the following morning they are stripped and washed, and dressed in their graduation clothes. They are carried, like babies, on the backs of their "mothers" up to the ruler's courtyard, where they dance *domba* for the last time as novices. Thenceforth they are ready for marriage and for fuller participation in Venda society. One function of the music and dance was to create a baby symbolically, and, as if to reinforce this, the bass drum is removed from the crossbar for the final rites.

There is an important relationship between the music of *domba* and of *tshikona*, which reflects the function of the two types of music in Venda society. A complete set of reed pipes is called *mutavha*. The word refers to the set and not to the number of tones to an octave. The same word is used to refer to a set of keys on the *mbira* and the xylophone. However, names are given to the notes in such a way that their relationships within the octave and their musical functions are recognized. The chief tone of a set of heptatonic reed pipes is called *phala*, and the tone an octave above it is called *phalana*, or "little *phala*." The tone above *phala* is called *thakhula*, the "lifter," because it leads the melody back down onto the chief tone. (It is functionally like a leading note in European music.) Every tone has a companion tone, a fifth below. This is not a device limited to *tshikona*: it is implicit in every Venda melody based on heptatonic modes. The companion tones in a pentatonic scale differ because of the spacing of the intervals, but the basically social principle that a tone must have a companion tone still applies, and it may be expressed explicitly in the "harmonies" improvised by other singers.

In instrumental music the interval of a tritone is permitted, but in vocal music it is avoided as a chord. An interesting contrast exists between *tshikona* and the *khulo* of *domba*, in which girls sing with their voices almost the same pattern that men play on their reed pipes (see Figure 8). The per-

mitted tritone is not in the same position in the pattern of
tshikona (*c"*/*f♯"* in 8a) as it would be in the pattern of *khulo*
(second chord in 8b), if it were not avoided. This is evidence
that *khulo* is *not* a simple transposition of *tshikona*: if it
were, the avoided tritone would appear, as in *tshikona*, in the

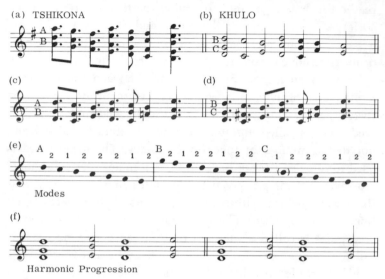

FIGURE 8. *Illustration of the transformation process by which*
khulo *is related to* tshikona, *and summary of modes and basic
chord sequence.*
(a) *The upper tones of* tshikona, *transposed down a semitone.*
(b) *The basic pattern of* khulo *for girls' voices.*
(c) *Transposition of* tshikona *to the same pitch as* khulo. *Note the*
f *natural and the position of the tritone.*
(d) *Transformation of* tshikona, *rewriting d" as* phala *instead of*
a". *Note how the position of the tritone differs from* tshikona *in*
8c, *but agrees with* khulo *in 8b.*
(e) *The three modes used in* tshikona *and* khulo, *rewritten without
accidentals.*
(f) *The harmonic basis of* khulo. *The sequence of chords also fits
the* tshikona *pattern, regardless of the different modes used.*
*Note: the figures indicate the number of semitones in the intervals
of the modes.*

penultimate, and not in the second chord. *Khulo* is, rather, a transformation that is generated by the different function of the music. Thus the companion tones of the men's *tshikona* (B in 8a, 8c, and 8e) have been selected as the chief mode of the girls' *khulo*, for which a further set of companion tones has been taken (C in 8b, 8d, and 8e). It is as if *tshikona* embodies within its *mutavha* a male and a female mode, and the male mode has been chosen for the men's music and the female mode for the girls' music. Both are united by their common relationship to a single basic harmonic progression (8f). Notice that in the harmonic progression there is a shift of tonal power from *phala* (*d"* in 8c, 8e, and 8f) to *thakhula* (*e"* in 8c, 8e, and 8f), and then back to *phala*. The relationship between the chords is determined by the fact that in the *tshikona* pattern every tone has two companion tones—the first a fifth below and the second a fifth above. Thus *d"/g'* and *e"/a'* are functionally "stronger" chords than *d"/a'* and *e"/b'* (see Figure 9).

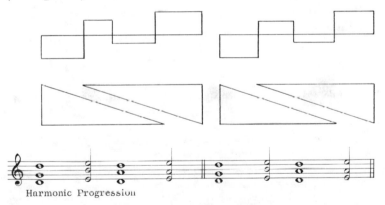

Harmonic Progression

FIGURE 9. *Diagram of the harmonic and tonal progressions of* tshikona *and* khulo, *showing how the power of* phala (d") *and* thakhula (e") *alters as they change their companion tones. The rectangles symbolize shifts of tonality, and the changing thickness of the "wedges" illustrates the decrease and increase of the tonal power of* phala *and* thakhula.

In spite of their different timbre and tempi, the musical affinity of *tshikona* and *khulo* ought to be apparent even to one who has no knowledge of Venda culture. To a certain extent the music speaks for itself. But, although the general nature of the relationship is clearly audible, the precise way in which this musical relationship has been achieved cannot possibly be derived from a study of the notes alone. The analysis must begin with the role of music in Venda society and culture (see Figures 5 and 7), so that we can see how patterns of culture and society have emerged in the shape of humanly organized sound.

Soundly
Organized
Humanity

*J*N THE FIRST CHAPTER I stated that, if we want to know how musical man is, we must be able to describe exactly what happens to any piece of music. In the second and third chapters I have tried to show why we shall never be able to do this until we understand what happens to the human beings who make the music. Music is a synthesis of cognitive processes which are present in culture and in the human body: the forms it takes, and the effects it has on people, are generated by the social experiences of human bodies in different cultural environments. Because music is humanly organized sound, it expresses aspects of the experience of individuals in society.

It follows that any assessment of human musicality must account for processes that are extramusical, and that these should be included in analyses of music. The answers to many important questions about musical structure may not be strictly musical. Why are certain scales, modes, and intervals preferred? The explanation may be historical, political, philosophical, or rational in terms of acoustical laws. What comes next when a certain musical pattern has been played? Is the next tone determined by the logic of the melodic pattern, or by a more general rule relating melody to patterns of speech tone, as in Venda music? Why should a pattern be repeated at a certain point? Why should it be repeated at all? Musicology must be able to answer these questions if it is to explain what is going on in music; but I believe that it will not succeed in answering general questions about music until it recognizes the peculiarities of different musical systems. Even the discoveries of systematic musicology may apply only to the musical traditions of systematic musicologists and to the perceptual faculties that have been developed in their own cultures.

I will reinforce this point with reference to four of the children's songs included in my book, *Venda Children's Songs* (Johannesburg: Witwatersrand University Press, 1967). This will show how an analysis of their sound alone is inadequate and misleading. We will consider the songs (Examples 22-25) first as "pure" music, then as sound organized in a particular cultural and social context.

Example 22

1. Po - ṭi - lo, 2. Ha - nga - la, 3. Ha - nga - la,

4. Nda te - ma, 5. Te - mi - so; 6. Tshi - ṇo - ni

7. Tsha ga - la 8. Mu - ta - nda. 9. Ma - ndu - le. 10. Gu - ni - wee!

Potilo seems to be based on ten half-note beats divided by the melody into 4+4+2, and incorporating thirty word-syllables which are grouped into threes as 1+1+2 eighth notes. One can imagine several ingenious explanations of the metrical structure of the song, which may or may not be correct; but the Venda who perform it are conscious of a single explanation, which is assigned by its cultural context. *Potilo* is a children's song (*luimbo lwa vhana*) in the subcategory of counting songs (*nyimbo dzu u vhala*): on each half-note beat, a finger is grasped and counted, from the left little finger to the thumb, and then through from the right thumb to the fourth finger, with a clap of the hands on the tenth half beat.

Example 23

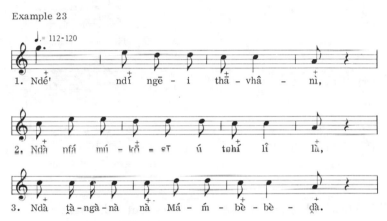

The second song, *Nde' ndi ngei thavhani*, uses five tones and is based on repetitions of four dotted quarter notes. In this case, we will consider not the meter but the changes in the melody. Again, a "purely" musical analysis will not do, because of the Venda system of relationships between speech tone and melody. The tonal sequence at the beginning of each phrase varies from GED to CED and CD, and there are different patterns in later repetitions of the basic melody. This may be heard as melodic variety that is balanced and pleasing to the ear, but it is not conceived musically. It is a consequence of changes in the speech tone of the different words, which in turn are generated by the "story" of the song (see also Figure 6). The form of the song is derived from a social model, so that the varying call and the unchanging response reflect a situation in which a soloist works with a chorus. Thus, speech-tone changes are reflected in the first, but not the second, section of each phrase, so that in the performance of a single person there is a condensation of a social situation which children will encounter when they grow up and participate in larger social groups.

Example 24

1. Thà-thà - thà! Thá-ngá dzí â   swá, Ndè' dzí â   swá:

2. Dzí á   swá nà Vhó-Má-rā - mbā   ná   Vhó-Nyú - ndò.

3. Vhó-Nyú - ndó vhé'   Rí   yà   'fhí?   Rì   yà shó-ndó - nì;

The third song also uses five tones, but a different arrangement of five tones. Notice the pattern EGCE, similar to that in *Potilo*, CEAC. This might be called a fanfare pattern; but bugles and fanfares are irrelevant in the context of traditional Venda culture. Again, the first part of the melody is like the call of call-response form, and there are minor variations of melody dependent on changes in speech tone. The same principles apply in the fourth song, which uses six tones and also has the "fanfare" pattern CEAC.

Example 25

1. Ndó   bvá   ná   tshì - dó - ngò   tshà ná   -   mà.

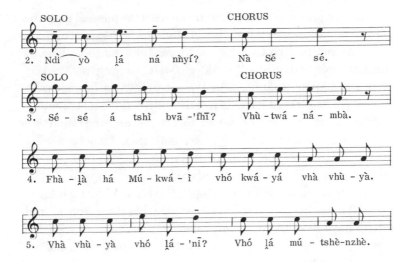

SOLO   CHORUS

2. Ndì yò ḷá ná nhyí?   Nà Sé - sé.

SOLO   CHORUS

3. Sé - sé á tshì bvā -'fhī?   Vhù - twá - ná - mbà.

4. Fhà - ḷà há Mú - kwá - ì vhó kwá - yá vhà vhù - yà.

5. Vhà vhù - yà vhó ḷá - 'nī?   Vhó ḷá mú - tshè-nzhè.

It could be argued that these four songs represent stages of musical evolution from a four-tone nucleus EDCA. It is possible to analyze them just as *musical* patterns, in terms of the iteration of tones and their convergence on tone centers, the rhythmic reinforcement of tones, tonic-dominant tonality, patterns of melodic relaxation and tension, and so on. If you treat these melodies as things in themselves, as "sonic objects," which is the kind of approach I am objecting to, you can work out several different analyses. This procedure is very common in analyses of European music and may be one of the reasons why musical journals are so full of contradictory explanations of the same music. Everyone disagrees hotly and stakes his academic reputation on what Mozart really meant in this or that bar of one of his symphonies, concertos, or quartets. If we knew exactly what went on inside Mozart's mind when he wrote them, there could be only one explanation.

If we analyze the four songs as music in culture, it seems that we can explain them without resort to arguments about musical evolution or the merits of alternative analyses. Furthermore, it is not necessary to concoct a theory that the songs are part of a musical *Gradus* by which children prepare for adult music, like Carl Orff's *Music for Children*. Two of the first songs that small children were singing in 1956-58 were the four-tone *Potilo* and the six-tone *Ndo bva na tshidongo* (Examples 22 and 25). They were the most popular children's songs, they belonged to classes of songs that are sung by boys and girls together, and they were generally learned before certain two- or three-tone songs that accompanied games children rarely played at an early age. Social factors tend to regulate the age at which Venda children learn the songs, and the fact that one has four tones, and others have five, six, or seven tones, has little to do with the learning process. It is the total pattern of the music and its associated situations which are more significant than the number of tones used in songs. Children learn these songs as they learn language, as complete ideas, and not gradually by musical progression.

The children's songs are the first music Venda children learn, in the sense of actively performing music. They are not the first music they hear, which is more likely to be the music of the national dance (*tshikona*), the premarital initiation dance (*domba*), or the many beer songs that will assail their ears as they are strapped to their mothers' backs. Other music that Venda boys hear and play is the music of the boys' dance (*tshikanganga*) and a series of associated reed-pipe dances for the pentatonic pipes (*nanga dza lutanga*).

Tshikona, the national dance, is played on different sets of heptatonic pipes. As I pointed out in the second and third chapters, it is the most important Venda music; and there is a close relationship between its musical form and its expressive purposes. The music of *tshikona* is such that if you ask a Venda to sing it, he may give one of several possible versions (see Figure 10). He may even attempt to give a more graphic representation in which snatches of vocal phrases

FIGURE 10. *Different ways in which the Venda may sing* tshikona, *their national dance for reed pipes and drums. The figures indicate the number of semitones in each interval.* D *and* E *are the nearest equivalents to a scale that the Venda sing: singers do not complete the octave, but pause on the seventh tone or repeat the pattern. The names of one octave of reed pipes are given. Tshikona is here transposed down a minor third.*

accompany an imitation of the pipes. All these variations, and many others, can be drawn from the *tshikona* pattern (see Figure 11a). All are transformations that are accepted by the Venda as *tshikona*. Figure 11 also shows how three of the children's songs (Examples 22, 24, and 25) may be derived from the *tshikona* pattern: the recurrence of the "fanfare" patterns suggests strongly that the relationship is not an imaginary creation of the music analyst. Besides, on one occasion a group of Venda boys actually converted *Thathatha* (Example 24) into *tshikona*, abandoning the words for sounds that are said to represent the sound of reed pipes, *fhe, fhe, fhe.*

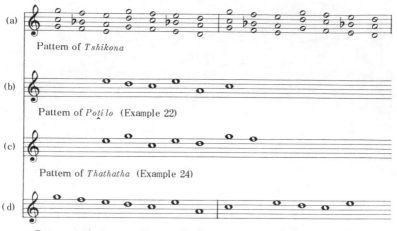

(a) Pattern of *Tshikona*

(b) Pattern of *Poṭi lo* (Example 22)

(c) Pattern of *Thathatha* (Example 24)

(d) Pattern of *Ndo bva na tshidongo* (Example 25)

FIGURE 11. *Relationship between the melodies of three Venda children's songs and the music of* tshikona, *only part of which is given, transposed down a minor third.*

Similarly, the song *Nde' ndi ngei thavhani* (Example 23) is related to the pattern of *Mutshaini* (see Figure 12a), which is one of the pentatonic reed-pipe melodies. The relationship of a four-tone song *Nandi Munzhedzi* (see Figure 12c) to another reed-pipe melody, *Mangovho* (see Figure 12b), shows how that song is *not* related to *tshikona*, as is *Poṭilo* (see Figure 11b), although both use the same tones. What reveals their relationship is the pattern of their melodies. Thus one four-tone song is derived from a pentatonic model and another is derived from a heptatonic model. The principles of transformation are the same, and the musical results are similar at the surface level, but their basic conceptual models are different. This is why I maintained above that the total pattern of a melody may be more significant than the number of tones used. An apparently elementary product may conceal a complex process, and vice versa.

There are many other songs that are related to *tshikona* and

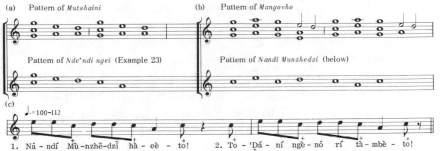

FIGURE 12. *Relationship between two Venda children's songs and two pentatonic reed-pipe melodies played by youths and boys (No. 4 in Figures 5 and 7).*

to the boys' reed-pipe dances, as I have demonstrated in my book. My point is that formal musicological analysis may become inadequate and even irrelevant as soon as the songs are analyzed in relation to other items of Venda music and in terms of the Venda music system, and also in relation to the social "origins" of that system. The children's songs are transformations of music that children must have heard and will almost certainly perform later in their lives. They have been condensed by a process of ellipsis not unlike that which occurs in the early speech of children. Instead of imitating a downward-moving, often heptatonic pattern of melody, they exhibit a new type of pattern, which happens to suit the more limited range of children's voices.

The processes of creation were probably unconscious; and it is even possible that the songs were originally composed by children. But if they were not, and they are now learned by conscious imitation rather than by osmosis, there was a time when they were composed, and the transformation process used was similar in principle to that which relates the pattern of *tshikona* to the *khulo* of *domba,* as discussed in chapter 3 (see Figure 8). The important point here is that the principles of the creative process cannot always be found in the surface structures of the music, and many of the generative factors are not musical. For instance, I also showed how a basic melody may be restructured to suit changes in the speech-tone patterns of words (see Figure 6). Even Venda children are able to set entirely new strings of words to an existing melody in a way that is recognized as characteristically Venda (see page 69), although they receive no formal instruction and the rules of the system can be derived only from a comparative analysis of many different songs. Creativity in Venda music depends on the use and transformation of the basic conceptual models that generate its surface structures; and because these models are acquired unconsciously as part of the maturation process, I do not think that they can be used really creatively by someone who is not deeply involved in Venda society.

In other words, the rules of Venda music are not arbitrary, like the rules of a game. In order to create new Venda music, you must *be* a Venda, sharing Venda social and cultural life from early childhood. The technical resources of Venda music may not seem very great to one accustomed to European classical music, and the basic rules of composition could probably be learned from a study of recordings and of my own analyses. But I am convinced that a trained musician could not compose music that was absolutely new and specifically Venda, and acceptable as such to Venda audiences, unless he had been brought up in Venda society. Because the composition of Venda music depends so much on being a Venda, and its structure is correspondingly related to that condition of being, it follows that an analysis of the sound cannot be conceived apart from its social and cultural context. The music of the four songs could have been analyzed in terms of their notes only, but such analyses would not have revealed the deep structures of the music, the processes by which they were created in the context of Venda society. A context-sensitive analysis turns out to be more general, because it explains the music of the children's songs according to a system that applies to other items of Venda music, and in terms of their respective social functions. That is, the social and expressive relationships between the function of the children's songs and the different reed-pipe dances in Venda society is reflected in their formal, musical relationships.

Analyses of music are essentially descriptions of sequences of different kinds of creative act: they should explain the social, cultural, psychological, and musical events in the lives of individuals and groups that lead to the production of organized sound. At the surface level, creativity in music is expressed chiefly in musical composition and in performance, in the organization of new relationships between sounds or new ways of producing them. Concern for the sound as an end in itself, or for the social means to the attainment of that end, are two aspects of musical creativity that cannot be separated, and both seem to be present in many societies. Whether the emphasis is on humanly organized sound or on soundly organized humanity, on a tonal experience related to people or a shared experience related to tones, the function of music is to reinforce, or relate people more closely to, certain experiences which have come to have meaning in their social life.

Musical creativity can be described in terms of social, musical, and cognitive processes. In two other published analyses of over one hundred Venda songs, I have drawn up six sets of rules that explain their patterns of sound. The first set, "social and cultural factors," begins with the rule 1.0.0. "Music is performed as part of a social situation." This may seem absurdly obvious, but it is a necessary prelude to more complex rules that explain musical patterns as products of their social antecedents. The next four sets are basically musical: "Tempo, meter, and rhythm," "Speech tone and melody," "Harmony and tonality," and "Musical development"; and the last is cognitive: "Transformation processes." These rules are clumsy and provisional, and they are inadequate because they assume a working knowledge of Venda culture and society. I shall not discuss them further, but I want to suggest how and why such rules could be generalized and refined in terms of a unified theory of cognition, society, culture, and creativity.

First, let me outline certain theoretical assumptions. Emile Durkheim, in *The Elementary Forms of the Religious Life* ([London: Allen and Unwin, 1968 (1915)], p. 447) argues that society is "not a nominal being created by reason, but a system of active forces." I believe that behavior is an integral part of an animal's constitution; that human beings are not infinitely plastic; and that we shall learn more about music and human musicality if we look for basic rules of musical behavior which are biologically, as well as culturally, conditioned and species-specific. It seems to me that what is ultimately of most importance in music cannot be learned like other cultural skills: it is there in the body, waiting to be brought out and developed, like the basic principles of language formation. You cannot really learn to improvise, but this does not mean that improvisation is random. The man who does it is not improvised: all aspects of his behavior are subject to a series of interrelated, structured systems, and, when he improvises, he is expressing these systems in relation to the reactions he picks up from his audience. Similarly, married Venda women do not relearn the music of *domba* every four or five years, when a new school is set up: they relive a social situation, and the right music emerges when that experience is shared under certain conditions of individuality in community.

The rules of musical behavior are not arbitrary cultural conventions, and techniques of music are not like developments in technology. Musical behavior may reflect varying degrees of consciousness of social forces, and the structure and function of music may be related to basic human drives and to the biological need to maintain a balance among them.

If the Venda perform communal music chiefly when their stomachs are full, it is not simply to kill time. If drives of cooperation, reproduction, and exploration are overlooked in the pursuit of self-preservation, the harmony of nature is disturbed. Man cannot be satisfied with having: he must also be, and become. But neither can he be, without having. When the Venda are hungry, or busy working to avoid hunger, they do not have the time or energy to make much music. Nor do they imagine that music might in some magical way alleviate their hunger, any more than their rain makers expect rain to fall before they have seen the insects whose movements precede it. The music is in them, but it requires special conditions to emerge. I suggest that the Venda make music when their stomachs are full because, consciously or unconsciously, they sense the forces of separation inherent in the satisfaction of self-preservation, and they are driven to restore the balance with exceptionally cooperative and exploratory behavior. Thus forces in culture and society would be expressed in humanly organized sound, because the chief function of music in society and culture is to promote soundly organized humanity by enhancing human consciousness.

In the third chapter I suggested that many formal changes in European music came about as a result of attempts by composers to make people more aware of social disharmony and inequality. Musical creativity was thus a function of composers' attitudes to the separation of people in societies which should have been fully cooperative. In much the same way, we may say that the thematic relationships of *tshikona* and the Venda children's songs express corresponding social relationships. *Tshikona* symbolized the largest society known to the Venda in the past; and because the oppression of *apartheid* restricts them in the larger society of which they are painfully aware, this traditional society still remains the largest in which they can move about with comparative freedom. *Tshikona* is universal both in content and in form: everyone attends it; it epitomizes the principle of individuality in community (like a Bach chorale, it is interesting for all performers, in contrast to the average hymn accompaniment which reduces altos and tenors to slaves of sopranos and basses); and its musical structure incorporates the most important features of Venda music. It is a shared experience, both socially and musically.

Venda children's songs are also universal, rather than parochial, in that every Venda child is expected to sing some of them and their performance is not limited to a cult group or social clique. Thus it is not surprising to find musical relationships between *tshikona* and the children's songs that parallel their social relationships. In the context of Venda social and musical life, the children's songs can be seen as "contrasting on the surface but identical in substance," as Rudolph Reti has described some great works of music in his book, *The Thematic Process in Music* ([London: Faber and Faber, 1961], p. 5).

It is tempting to see the basic musical form of theme and variation as an expression of social situations and social forces transformed according to patterns of culture and the state of the division of labor in society. Thus the essential differences between music in one society and another may be social and not musical. If English music may seem to be more complex than Venda music and practiced by a smaller number of people, it is because of the consequences of the division of labor in society, and not because the English are less musical or their music is cognitively more complex. There are not more or less things for an individual to learn in different societies, and in the context of each culture they are not basically more or less difficult. There are more or fewer different fields in which to learn. It is neither easier nor more difficult to be a Bushman than an American. It is different.

As a result of the division of labor in society, some people must do things for others. If I were a Bushman I would have made my own clothes and I would hunt for my own food: I would really be an individual in a way no American can be. (Americans who opt out and live a folksy or utopian life are not really escaping the division of labor in their society. Because of the protection of the larger society they enjoy an easy life that has almost nothing in common with the lives of peasants and tribesmen who cannot afford the luxuries they take for granted, and they try to avoid the problems of collective responsibility with which the more extensive division of labor presents them.)

In any society, cultural behavior is learned; although the introduction of new skills may represent an intellectual break-through, the learning of accumulated skills does not present essentially different or more difficult tasks to the members of different cultures. If there is a pattern to the difference, it is that Americans have to learn more about less. This means th they must learn less than the Bushmen about some things. Problems in human societies begin when people learn less about love, because love is the basis of our existence as human beings. Kierkegaard has expressed this in the following words:

One generation can learn much from another, but that which is purely human no generation can learn from the preceding generation. In this respect every generation begins again from the beginning, possessing no other tasks but those of preceding generations and going no further, unless the preceding generation has betrayed itself and deceived itself. . . . No generation has learned how to love from another, no generation begins at any other point than the beginning, and no subsequent generation has a shorter task than the generation which preceded it [*Fear and Trembling* (London and New York: Oxford University Press, 1939), pp. 183-84].

The hard task is to love, and music is a skill that prepares man for this most difficult task. Because in this respect every generation has to begin again from the beginning, many composers feel that their task is to write new music not as if they were designing a new model of automobile, but as if they were assessing the human situation in which new automobiles are made and used. The task of designing new automobiles is basically a technical and commercial problem that may be compared to writing incidental music in the style of Tchaikovsky, Mahler, or Debussy. Provided a person is brought up in a certain social class, with adequate emotional opportunities, writing music in the style of Tchaikovsky could be learned without great effort and carried on from one generation to another, like many other cultural skills. Although a composer might have the greatest respect for Tchaikovsky's music, if he were aware of and concerned with the contemporary task of being human and wanted to say something about it in his music, he could not reproduce that sort of music in a society whose tasks are different from Tchaikovsky's. (Stravinsky's *Le Baiser de la Fée* may have begun as a rehash of Tchaikovsky, but it turns out as pure Stravinsky, and essentially a new work.) Thus if a composer wants to produce music that is relevant to his contemporaries, his chief problem is not really musical, though it may seem to him to be so: it is a problem of attitude to contemporary society and culture in relation to the basic human problem of learning to be human. Music is not a language that describes the way society seems to be, but a metaphorical expression of feelings associated with the way society really is. It is a reflection of and response to social forces, and particularly to the consequences of the division of labor in society.

Some music expresses the actual solidarity of groups when people come together and produce patterns of sound that are signs of their group allegiances; and other music expresses theoretical solidarity when a composer brings together patterns of sound that express aspects of social experience. Just as diverse social groups in, say, Venda society may be brought together by a performance of their national dance, so in an industrial society contrasting patterns of sound may be brought together by a composer through the single idea, and corresponding thematic unity, of a symphony. Just as a Venda chief said to me, "You shall hear the finest performance imaginable of our national dance: I will call to my capital every available player in the district," so Mahler said, "To write a symphony means, to me, to construct a world with all the tools of the available technique."

Relationships between formal and expressive analyses of music can be established even in matters such as the quality of creativity, an issue that constantly occupies musicologists and critics. In recent years, creative ability has been assessed in terms of a composer's ability to produce thematic unity with expressive contrast, and the impressive studies of Heinrich Schenker, Rudolph Reti, Hans Keller, Alan Walker, and others have tended to stress that this may often be an unconscious process. For example, Alan Walker has shown how the themes of Tchaikovsky's Fourth Symphony spring from the opening "fate theme," which the composer recognized intuitively as the germ of the entire symphony (A Study in Musical Analysis [London: Barrie and Rockliff, 1962], pp. 116-26). Many critics have dismissed this symphony as poorly constructed on the grounds that its thematic material is not treated as it ought to be according to the conventional rules of symphonic construction. The work could be described as an intellectual leap forward, in that Tchaikovsky was led to a new way of working out symphonic form; and it is interesting that the musical consequences of this basically human achievement are appreciated intuitively by lay audiences, though poorly understood by the closed minds of some musical experts.

The theories of Rudolph Reti and his followers match well with recent research that has shown that the ability to think creatively and to construct new forms is a function of personality. Creativity requires breadth of view, or what Milton Rokeach calls an "open mind," and the ability to synthesize is a critically important factor. People with open minds, who are low in ethnocentricism, reveal a comprehensive cognitive organization, which is potentially more creative than the narrower cognitive organization exhibited by people with closed minds. (I should add that surface ethnocentricism should not always be taken as evidence of real ethnocentricism. For example, in South Africa the surface ethnocentricism of blacks who see a form of Black Power as the only means of regaining their land and freedom is very different from the ethnocentricism of the whites who oppose them.)

There is evidence which suggests that, although human creativity may appear to be the result of individual effort, it is in fact a collective effort that is expressed in the behavior of individuals. Originality may be an expression of innate exploratory behavior with the accumulated materials of a cultural tradition; and the ability to synthesize, which is often said to distinguish genius from talent, may express the comprehensive cognitive organization that is generated by experience of the relationships that exist between the social groups who use and develop the techniques of the tradition. If this is so—and I am convinced that it is true—differences in cultures and developments in technology are the result of differences not of intellect, but of human organization. If the whites of South Africa seem to perform better than the blacks, or the rich and elite of a country seem to perform better than the poor or the masses, it is not because they or their parents are cleverer or have a richer cultural heritage: it is because their society is organized in such a way that they have better opportunities to develop their human potential, and consequently their cognitive organization. If intelligence tests devised by members of a certain class show poor performance by the members of another class in a theoretically "open" society, we should first ask just how open the society is and consider to what degree its class divisions may inhibit the cognitive development of its less fortunate members.

Changes and developments in culture and society are a function of population growth and of people's relationships and attitudes within given populations. Greater productivity has been achieved by larger groups of people involved in joint enterprises. In such cases, an increase in the division of labor is dynamically productive, but only when it is not also a division of people. The interaction of minds developed under different conditions is a stimulus to invention in a new, shared situation, provided that the situation really is shared. If a shared situation becomes static or formalized, or disintegrates altogether, it follows that creativity will tend to dry up, and it will become increasingly hard for members of a society to adapt to the changes that must result inevitably from the birth, life, and death of its individuals. It sometimes happens that remarkable cultural developments can take place in societies in which man's humanity is progressively abused, restricted, and disregarded. This is because cultural development can reach a stage where it is almost mechanically self-generative—but only in certain fields and for a limited time. The history of many civilizations has shown that a society and its culture may ultimately collapse because of human alienation. The machine runs down without the only power that can change it, the creative force that springs from human self-consciousness. This is why the Venda stress that "man is man because of his asociations with other men," and reinforce their belief with music. When they share the experience of an invisible conductor in their drumming and singing and pipe playing, they become more aware of society's system of active forces, and their own consciousness is enhanced.

Music cannot change societies, as can changes in technology and political organization. It cannot make people act unless they are already socially and culturally disposed to act. It cannot instill brotherhood, as Tolstoy hoped, or any other state or social value. If it can do anything to people, the best that it can do is to confirm situations that already exist. It cannot in itself generate thoughts that may benefit or harm mankind, as some writers have suggested; but it can make people more aware of feelings that they have experienced, or partly experienced, by reinforcing, narrowing or expanding their consciousness in a variety of ways. Since music is learned in these kinds of context, it is composed in the same spirit. A person may create music for financial gain, for private pleasure, for entertainment, or to accompany a variety of social events, and he need not express overt concern for the human condition. But his music cannot escape the stamp of the society that made its creator human, and the kind of music he composes will be related to his consciousness of, and concern for, his fellow human beings. His cognitive organization will be a function of his personality.

Now those who are concerned with musicology and ethnomusicology may be disappointed, because I seem to suggest that there are no grounds for comparing different musical systems; there is no possibility of any universal theory of musical behavior, and no hope of cross-cultural communication. But if we consider our own experiences, we must realize that this is not in fact so. Music *can* transcend time and culture. Music that was exciting to the contemporaries of Mozart and Beethoven is still exciting, although we do not share their culture and society. The early Beatles' songs are still exciting although the Beatles have unfortunately broken up. Similarly, some Venda songs that must have been composed hundreds of years ago still excite the Venda, and they also excite me. Many of us are thrilled by *koto* music from Japan, *sitar* music from India, Chopi xylophone music, and so on. I do not say that we receive the music in exactly the same way as the players (and I have already suggested that even the members of a single culture do not receive their own music in the same ways), but our own experiences suggest that there are some possibilities of cross-cultural communication. I am convinced that the explanation for this is to be found in the fact that at the level of deep structures in music there are elements that are common to the human psyche, although they may not appear in the surface structures.

Consider the matter of "feeling in music," which is often invoked to distinguish two technically correct performances of the same piece. This doctrine of feeling is in fact based on the recognition of the existence and importance of deep structures in music. It asserts that music stands or falls by virtue of what is heard and how people respond to what they hear "in the notes," but it assumes that the surface relationships between tones which may be perceived as "sonic objects" are only part of other systems of relationships. Because the assumptions are not clearly stated and are only dimly understood, the assertions become all the more dogmatic and are often clothed in the language of an elitist sect. The effect of this confusion on musically committed people can be traumatic, and the musically inclined may be discouraged altogether.

When, as a boy, I mastered a technically difficult piece of piano music, I was sometimes told that I played without feeling. As a result of this I tended to play more loudly or aggressively, or to fold up altogether. It seemed as if an assault was being made on my integrity as a person, rather than on my technical ability. In fact, my "unfeeling" performance was the result of inadequate, hit-or-miss techniques of teaching in a society whose educational theory was founded on a confused doctrine relating success to a combination of superior inheritance, hard work, and moral integrity. A snobbish distaste for technical expertise, technology, and "mere" craftsmanship discouraged attention to basic mechanical problems unless they were wrapped up in an aura of morality —as was the diligent practice of scales and arpeggios. The Venda attitude toward playing well is essentially technical and not ego-deflating. When the rhythm of an alto drum in *domba* is not quite right, the player may be told to move in such a way that her beat is part of a total body movement: she plays with feeling precisely because she is shown how to experience the physical feeling of moving with her instrument and in harmony with the other drummers and dancers. There is no suggestion that she is an insensitive or inadequate person. What is a commonplace of Venda musical instruction seems to be a rarity in "my" society.

So often, the expressive purpose of a piece of music is to be found through identification with the body movements that generated it, and these in turn may have their origins in culture as much as in the peculiarities of an individual. There are so many different tempi in the world of nature and the body of man that music has endless possibilities of physical coordination with any one of them, or several of them together. Without this kind of coordination, which can be learned only by endless experimentation, or more quickly by direct aural transmission, there is little possibility that music will be *felt*. When we know the associated dance step, we may know whether ♫ ♫ ♫ ♫♪ should be thought of as 1-2-3-123, 1231-2-3-, or 1-2-3-4, or whatever. It may be necessary to slow down one's breathing in order to "feel" a piece of Korean music, whose unique elegance and refinement are hard for a European to appreciate. A similar control of the body makes it easier to catch the *innigster empfindung* of Beethoven's Piano Sonata, Op. 109, last movement. Just breathe slowly, relax the body completely and play—and the *empfindung* comes through the body. It is no longer an elusive, mysterious Teutonic quality!

Obviously the most deeply felt performance of any piece of music will be that which approaches most closely the feelings of its creator when he began to capture the force of his individual experience with musical form. Since this experience may often begin as a rhythmical stirring of the body, it may be possible for a performer to recapture the right feeling by finding the right movement. Is it surprising, then, that many people abandon music because they cannot play what they feel, or cannot feel what they play? By creating a false dichotomy between the deep and surface structures of music, many industrial societies have taken away from people much of the practice and pleasure of music making. What is the use of teaching a pianist to play scales and arpeggios according to some didactic system, and then expecting him to *feel* the piano music of Mozart, Beethoven, Chopin, Debussy, and Ravel by a separate effort of the will, or the employment of some mysterious spiritual attribute? Exercise of the finger muscles is one thing, but the scales and arpeggios of a composer's music will perhaps be felt most deeply when they are played according to *his* system. That is, if you find out by feeling for it how Debussy might have held his hands and body when he played the piano, you might get a better feeling for his music. You might find that you could play the music with feeling without having to be immensely "deep."

In fact you would be profoundly deep, because you would be sharing the most important thing about music, that which is in the human body and which is universal to all men. It would be mysterious only in so far that we do not understand what happens in the remarkable bodies all human beings possess. It would *not* be mysterious in the sense of being something for only a chosen few.

Perhaps there is a hope of cross-cultural understanding after all. I do not say that we can experience exactly the same thoughts associated with bodily experience; but to feel with the body is probably as close as anyone can ever get to resonating with another person. I shall not attempt to discuss the issue of musical communication as a physiological phenomenon; but if music begins, as I have suggested, as a stirring of the body, we can recall the state in which it was conceived by getting into the body movement of the music and so feeling it very nearly as the composer felt it. Some may be fortunate enough to be able to do this intuitively; but for most people it will be easier if the notes of music are regarded as the product of cognitive, physical, and social processes.

I would like to consider again the examples of *tshikona* and the children's songs. I am no longer satisfied with the analysis I gave in *Venda Children's Songs*. I tried to explain musical phenomena as expressions of social situations; but I no longer consider this to be sufficiently general. For example, the use of the terms call and response implies a socially derived musical form, rather than seeking a basic structure from which both responsorial form and solo-chorus/leader-follower social situations may be derived. Suppose we look at the social, musical, economic, legal, and other subsystems of a culture as transformations of basic structures that are in the body, innate in man, part of his biological equipment; then we may have different explanations for a lot of things that we have taken for granted, and we may be able to see correspondences between apparently disparate elements in social life. For example, the following relationships may be transformations of a single structure: call/response, tone/companion tone, tonic/countertonic, individual/community, chief/subjects, theme/variation, male/female, and so forth.

Ethnomusicology is in some respects a branch of cognitive anthropology. There seem to be universal structural principles in music, such as the use of mirror forms (see Example 16, for instance), theme and variation, repetition, and binary form. It is always possible that these may arise from experience of social relations or of the natural world: an unconscious concern for mirror forms may spring from the regular experience of mirror forms in nature, such as observation of the two "halves" of the body. If different aspects and fields of human behavior are analyzed in this way, we may have a new view of human societies and human "progress," and a new concept of the future of man, which is most important.

The evolution of technology and an increase in the size of societies cannot then be taken as signs of the evolution of culture in general, or of man's intellectual potential. An African "folk" song is not necessarily less intellectual than a symphony: the apparent simplicity of sound produced may conceal complex processes of generation; it may have been stimulated by an intellectual leap forward in which its composer saw beyond the boundaries of his culture and was able to invent a powerful new form to express in sound his vision of the unlimited possibilities of human development. As a human achievement, this would be more significant than the surface complexity of a classroom symphony produced in the context of a technologically advanced society, and so comparable to an original masterpiece. And, like a symphonic masterpiece, it might survive because of its musical quality and what it means to critical listeners.

Through the operations of the brain, three orders of consciousness are working at the same time in one person's body: the universal, automatic complexity of the natural world; group consciousness, which has been learned through the shared experience of cultural life; and individual consciousness, which may transcend the boundaries of group consciousness when an individual uses or develops areas of basic automatic complexity which have not been explored by his society. I use the term "group consciousness" deliberately, because I regard the more generalized "social consciousness" as an aspect of individual consciousness. There is an important difference between an individual's "natural" awareness of any man next to him as a human neighbor, and his "cultural" awareness of neighbors as people who speak certain languages or belong to certain races, classes, or creeds. Because human beings are physiologically parts of the natural world, I doubt if they can create anything whose principles are not already inherent in the system of automatic complexity to which they belong. Computers, radios, X-ray photography, and television are in a sense no more than extensions and props to man's inborn powers of calculation, telepathy, sensory diagnosis, and clairvoyance. Inventions may be described as purposeful discoveries of situations that are already possible by means that already exist. I would modify the hypothesis that "man makes himself" by suggesting that through the centuries of cultural achievement man has extended himself in the world, and has developed the expression of his consciousness of the world. He has devised experiments in living that may help him better to be what he already is. I am not claiming that cultures in themselves are genetically inherited, but that they are generated by processes that are acquired biologically and developed through social interaction.

An analysis of the deeper processes of Venda musical behavior suggests that some innate capacities are as necessary as are experiences of learning for realizing even elementary musical ability, let alone exceptional musical ability. The most convincing evidence of innate creative capacities is to be found in the ways the Venda apply themselves to new experiences of sonic order, and in the processes that have generated different features of their musical tradition and constantly generate the variations within that tradition. The Venda adoption and adaptation of European music is testimony to the unconscious, creative application of musical processes. The so-called "mistakes" in their singing of European music may sometimes be due to inadequate learning facilities, but they may also be intentional. The Venda are able to imitate chromatic intervals or sharpened leading notes or European chord sequences; but they generally prefer to create rather than imitate, and they choose to ignore these European features or even improve on them—not because they are bound to learned patterns of behavior, but because there are deeper processes at work in their music making, which inspire a creative adaptation of the new sounds they hear. I am not arguing that particular musical systems are innate, but that some of the processes that generate them may be innate in all men and so species-specific. Similar evidence of creativity may be found in Venda children's songs, many of which may have been composed by children. Their structures suggest a creative use of features of the musical system which extends beyond techniques that might have been learned in society. I do not see how the deeper, apparently unconscious processes of generation could have been taught or learned in society except through a whole complicated process of relationships between innate potentialities and the realization of these in culture through social interaction.

If we study music in the ways I have suggested, we ought to be able to learn something about structures of human interaction in general by way of the structures involved in the creation of music, and so learn more about the inner nature of man's mind. One of the advantages of studying music is that it is a relatively spontaneous and unconscious process. It may represent the human mind working without interference, and therefore observation of musical structures may reveal some of the structural principles on which all human life is based. If we can show exactly how musical behavior (and, perhaps, all aspects of human behavior in culture) is generated by finite sets of rules applied to an infinite number of variables, we shall learn not only what aspects of musical behavior are specifically musical, but also how and when these rules and variables may be applied in other kinds of human behavior.

By learning more about the automatic complexity of the human body, we may be able to prove conclusively that all men are born with potentially brilliant intellects, or at least a very high degree of cognitive competence, and that the source of cultural creativity is the consciousness that springs from social cooperation and loving interaction. By discovering precisely how music is created and appreciated in different

social and cultural contexts, and perhaps establishing that
musicality is a universal, species-specific characteristic, we
can show that human beings are even more remarkable than
we presently believe them to be—and not just a few human
beings, but all human beings—and that the majority of us
live far below our potential, because of the oppressive nature
of most societies. Armed with this vital information about
the minds of men, we can begin to discredit forever the myths
about the "stupidity" of the majority and the supposedly
"innate" selfishness and aggressiveness of man, which are
peddled all the time by people who use them to justify the
coercion of their fellow men into undemocratic social systems.

In a world in which authoritarian power is maintained by
means of superior technology, and the superior technology is
supposed to indicate a monopoly of intellect, it is necessary
to show that the real sources of technology, of all culture, are
to be found in the human body and in cooperative interaction
between human bodies. Even falling in love may be more
significant as a cognitive activity in which learned categories
are realigned, than as an exertion of the sex organs or a
hormonal reaction. In a world such as ours, in this world of
cruelty and exploitation in which the tawdry and the mediocre
are proliferated endlessly for the sake of financial profit, it is
necessary to understand why a madrigal by Gesualdo or a
Bach Passion, a *sitar* melody from India or a song from
Africa, Berg's *Wozzeck* or Britten's *War Requiem*, a Balinese
gamelan or a Cantonese opèra, or a symphony by Mozart,
Beethoven, or Mahler, may be profoundly necessary for
human survival, quite apart from any merit they may have as
examples of creativity and technical progress. It is also necessary to explain why, under certain circumstances, a "simple"
"folk" song may have more human value than a "complex"
symphony.

JOHN BLACKING is professor of social anthropology at the Queen's University of Belfast, Northern Ireland. In 1970 he was appointed professor of anthropology at Western Michigan University, where he first taught courses in anthropology and ethnomusicology in 1971.

Born in England on October 22, 1928, he was educated at Salisbury Cathedral and Sherborne schools, where he received his early musical training. During a period of compulsory military service, he was commissioned in H.M. Coldstream Guards and spent the year 1948-49 in Malaya. He learned the Malay language and, while on military operations in the jungle, visited settlements of the Sakai and Senoi tribesmen who lived there. These experiences, together with many encounters with Malay, Chinese, and Indian people and their cultures, changed the direction of his career and forced a gradual reassessment of his own culture and its values.

In 1953, Dr. Blacking graduated from King's College, Cambridge, with a bachelor's degree in social anthropology. During the summer of 1952 he had studied ethnomusicology at the Musée de l'Homme, Paris, under André Schaeffner. An appointment as Government Adviser on Aborigines in

Malaya lasted six days, until he was dismissed after a disagreement with General Sir Gerald Templer in November 1953. Thereafter, he did some anthropological research, taught at a secondary school in Singapore, broadcast on Radio Malaya, accompanied Maurice Clare on a concert tour, returned to Paris for piano lessons in June 1954, and went to South Africa as musicologist of the International Library of African Music.

He worked with Dr. Hugh Tracey on recording tours in Zululand and Moçambique, and transcribed and analyzed music in the library's collection. During 1956-58 he undertook fieldwork among the Venda of the Northern Transvaal, and in 1959 he was appointed lecturer in social anthropology and African government at the University of the Witwatersrand, Johannesburg. He was awarded his doctorate by the university in 1965, and at the end of the year appointed professor and head of the department. In 1965, he was also visiting professor of African Music at Makerere University, Kampala. In 1966, he was appointed chairman of the African Studies Programme at the University of the Witwatersrand, and at the end of 1969 he left South Africa.

Dr. Blacking has carried out ethnomusicological fieldwork among the Gwembe Tonga and Nsenga of Zambia, and in parts of Uganda and South Africa, as well as anthropological research in and around Johannesburg. He is the author of many publications on Venda initiation rites and music and on the relationship between the patterns of music and culture. Among his publications are two long-playing records of Nsenga music, *Black Background: The Childhood of a South African Girl*, *Venda Children's Songs: A Study in Ethnomusicological Analysis*, and *Process and Product in Human Society*.